Inspiring | Educating | Creating | Entertaining

Brimming with creative inspiration, how-to projects, and useful information to enrich your everyday life, Quarto.com is a favorite destination for those pursuing their interests and passions.

First Published in 2023 by The Harvard Common Press, an imprint of The Quarto Group, 100 Cummings Center, Suite 265-D, Beverly, MA 01915, USA.
T (978) 282-9590 F (978) 283-2742 Quarto.com

The Harvard Common Press titles are also available at discount for retail, wholesale, promotional, and bulk purchase. For details, contact the Special Sales Manager by email at specialsales@quarto.com or by mail at The Quarto Group, Attn: Special Sales Manager, 100 Cummings Center, Suite 265-D, Beverly, MA 01915, USA.

26 25 24 23 22   1 2 3 4 5

ISBN: 978-0-7603-7735-2

Digital edition published in 2023
eISBN: 978-0-7603-7736-9

Library of Congress Control Number: 2022942515

Design: Cindy Samargia Laun
Cover Image and photography: Jennifer Danella

Printed in China

Easy, Everyday Meals
for Hunters and Their Families

THE WEEKNIGHT
WILD
GAME
COOKBOOK

JENN DANELLA

HARVARD
COMMON
PRESS

CONTENTS

Introduction 6

1 Breakfast and Brunch 9

2 Appetizers and Tailgate Food 31

3 Soups, Stews, and Slow-Cooked Meals 63

4 Baked and Fried 99

5 Grilled and Griddled 133

6 Butchery 179

Acknowledgments 188
About the Author 189
Index 190

INTRODUCTION

Hello! My name is Jenn. I am a self-taught chef, hunter, angler, and author. I grew up in the suburbs of Pennsylvania, where my father raised me to love the outdoors. He had me fishing pretty much as soon as I could walk on my own and is also largely responsible for my love for hunting—by taking me out to hunt while I was in high school. Some of my fondest memories with him involve the outdoors, and I feel blessed to be able to have done these things at such a young age. This goes hand in hand with getting home from the hunt. My mother would always make the most of the meat, and thus my interest in cooking delicious meals started at a young age as well. She and I would get together almost every night and try new recipes. Our running joke was that I was the daughter who was always hungry and always asking, "What's for dinner?" I never imaged these two joys would continue to be such a big part of my life to this day.

FROM THEN TO NOW

So, how did I get to where I am today? Right after I finished college, my life became completely immersed in the outdoors. Hunting and fishing consumed all of my free time. I eventually moved away from home to live with my better half, Hunter, who has helped me become the successful outdoorswoman I am today. Together, we've traveled all over North America in search of wild game and new adventures.

But really, I can also trace part of my adult life back to a photo from a goose hunt I posted online. That photo got shared on a large social media page and quickly my phone started buzzing. Follower after follower poured in. I did not realize at the time that this would be the start of something big. Each hunt, I continued to share my adventures. The more I shared, the more my page grew. Soon, I had over 100,000 followers. It still amazes me to this day that that many people are interested in the lifestyle I live. Now, I try to use my social media page to showcase hunting and fishing in a positive light, to help bring newcomers to the sport. My motivation stems from the ability to encourage women and younger generations to get into the great outdoors. I am forever appreciative to see my audience expand day after day.

HUNTING AND FISHING

At the heart of my passion is the wonder of catching or killing your own food and turning it into a delicious natural meal. It is a privilege many people don't understand today. Hunting, to me, not only feeds the body; it also feeds the soul. There is a different level of appreciation when you get to take part in every step of preparing your food—including the butchery.

When it comes to hunting, I like to try it all. Whether its hunting big game, wild turkey, waterfowl, or small game, you can count me in! Hunting with a bow is one of my favorites. In my eyes, there is no heart-pounding rush like having a target buck within 20 yards (18 m).

I also spend a lot of time with my hunting dogs. My lab, Little Katie, tags along on all of my waterfowl hunts and upland bird hunts. She retrieves anything from small mourning doves to big Canada geese and loves to do it. My beagles, Remington and Beretta, run the show when it comes to rabbit hunting. It is incredible to watch a dog work as they were bred to do. Nothing compares to the quiet companionship of a dog that understands your every command and can be a partner in your hunting adventures.

FROM THE FIELD TO THE KITCHEN

When it comes to making wild game recipes, I love making approachable dishes the whole family can enjoy. Being a self-taught chef, my meals are always focused on dishes that are achievable by the average home cook on the first try. I believe that food brings people together and that meals are meant to be at the table surrounded by family and friends. You don't need something to be fancy or to take forever to cook to make a memorable meal.

As I started writing and creating my own wild game recipes, however, I found that there weren't as many of these accessible, family-friendly recipes as there were for traditional meat. I could find plenty of recipes that were complicated, or even worse, tried to "hide" the flavor of wild game. But where were the weeknight meals, the kind that were my favorite ones to make and to eat?!

Over the years, I've made it my mission to develop these missing recipes. I want to show everyone that cooking with wild game is no more difficult than cooking with other meats—and just as delicious. That means teaching how to incorporate these lesser-known meats into popular dishes, from childhood favorites like cordon bleu and enchiladas to pub and game-day recipes like sliders and queso dip.

While I was writing this book, I included a handful of my all-time most popular dishes, like Slow Cooker Venison Barbacoa (page 91) and Venison Cheeseburger Egg Rolls with Special Sauce (page 53). But I also did a ton of recipe development. I wanted to give hunters and wild game lovers fun and exciting recipe ideas, simple and quick dinners in a pinch, and of course, some fresh takes on the classics. Whether you're looking for an easy slow-cooker meal like venison and stout stew or an epic feast from the grill like a reverse-seared venison backstrap, I wanted this book to have you covered.

For those ready to go further, I've also included a chapter with complete step-by-step instructions for venison butchery. It's not easy, but with some practice, I think you'll find it's well worth the effort.

No matter where you are on your hunting or cooking journey, I hope this book provides you with some inspiration and some exciting new meals that celebrate the work you (or a family member or friend) put into hunting and butchering the meat. Let's get cooking!

—*Jenn Danella*

BREAKFAST AND BRUNCH

Venison and Bacon Breakfast Pizza 13

Venison Quiche 15

Sunrise Venison Enchiladas.. 17

Venison Brunch Burger... 19

Country-Style Biscuits with Venison Gravy 21

Venison Breakfast Skillet.................................... 23

Honey Butter Pheasant Biscuit 25

Chorizo-Inspired Wild Hog Egg Bites 29

VENISON AND BACON BREAKFAST PIZZA

Although it is not traditionally considered the first meal of the day, pizza for breakfast just works. I mean, I guess it shouldn't be a surprise because who doesn't love pizza?! With a classic pizza crust, fresh eggs, ground venison, and of course, cheese, even the leftover slices will be a great way to start your day.

Yield: 6 servings

½ pound (225 g) ground venison

¼ teaspoon kosher salt

¼ teaspoon black pepper

½ teaspoon dried basil

4 bacon slices, chopped

1½ tablespoons (12 g) all-purpose flour

1 can (13.8 ounces, or 391 g) refrigerated classic pizza crust

1½ tablespoons (25 ml) extra-virgin olive oil

2 garlic cloves, minced

8 ounces (225 g) shredded mozzarella cheese

3 large eggs

2 tablespoons (8 g) chopped fresh parsley, for garnish

¼ teaspoon crushed red pepper, for garnish

1 Preheat the oven to 450°F (230°C, or gas mark 8). Lightly coat a baking sheet with olive oil.

2 Heat a large skillet over medium-high heat. Add the ground venison and then season with salt and pepper and add the basil. Cook until browned, about 10 minutes. Add the bacon and cook until just golden. Drain the excess fat. Transfer the venison and bacon to a paper towel–lined plate and set aside.

3 Working on a surface that has been sprinkled with flour, roll out the pizza dough into a 12-inch (30 cm) diameter round. Transfer to the prepared baking sheet.

4 Brush the dough with olive oil and garlic. Top with the mozzarella cheese, bacon, and venison, leaving three 3-inch (7.5 cm) circles for the eggs.

5 Place into the oven and bake until the edges begin to brown, about 10–12 minutes.

6 Remove from the oven and add the eggs. Crack the eggs gently to keep the yolks intact.

7 Place back into the oven and bake until the egg whites have set and the crust is golden brown, an additional 8–10 minutes.

8 Serve immediately, garnished with chopped fresh parsley and crushed red pepper, if desired.

VENISON QUICHE

I like to think of quiche as an egg-based pie that has nearly no rules. To make my take on a breakfast classic, you take piecrust and fill it with ground venison, bacon, onion, eggs, and a blend of cheddar and Gruyère cheese. While my recipe features ground venison, you can swap that out for another meat. As long as you keep the egg and cheese ratios intact, this recipe is super flexible. Be sure to let this dish cool for at least 30 minutes before serving to allow it to settle and firm up a bit.

Yield: 6–8 servings

1 tablespoon (14 g) butter or (15 ml) vegetable or peanut oil

4 ounces (115 g) ground venison

¼ teaspoon salt

¼ teaspoon black pepper

4 slices thick-cut bacon, chopped

½ sweet onion, finely diced

1 unbaked piecrust

½ cup (60 g) grated Gruyère cheese

½ cup (60 g) grated sharp cheddar cheese

1 cup (120 ml) heavy cream

6 large eggs

½ teaspoon dried thyme

½ teaspoon garlic powder

1 Preheat the oven to 375°F (190°C, or gas mark 5).

2 In a large skillet over medium-high heat, melt 1 tablespoon (14 g) of butter or (15 ml) oil. Add the ground venison and cook for about 7 minutes until the meat is just about browned. Add the salt, pepper, bacon, and onion. Sauté for 5 minutes. Remove from the pan using a slotted spoon and transfer to a paper towel–lined plate.

3 Place the piecrust in a pie dish. Spread the venison, bacon, and onion mixture into the bottom of the crust and sprinkle with the Gruyère and cheddar cheeses.

4 Next, whisk together the heavy cream and eggs in a medium-sized bowl.

5 Pour the egg and cream mixture over the filling in the crust and top with the thyme and garlic powder.

6 Bake the quiche for about 30 minutes until set and golden.

7 Allow to cool for 30 minutes prior to serving.

SUNRISE VENISON ENCHILADAS

. . . .

Okay, so you may have had breakfast pizza before or even chilaquiles. But what about breakfast enchiladas? In this recipe, you start with ground venison that gets seasoned with salt, chili powder, cayenne, and black pepper to give it a little kick. Then, the scrambled eggs and salsa come in, teaming up with the venison for the filling for the tortillas. You roll them up and place them on a bed of salsa verde and top them with enchilada sauce and cheese. After less than 30 minutes in the oven, you have a golden and bubbly breakfast that can easily feed a crowd.

Yield: 8 servings

1 pound (455 g) ground venison

1 poblano pepper, diced

½ teaspoon salt

½ teaspoon chili powder

¼ teaspoon cayenne pepper

¼ teaspoon black pepper

½ cup (130 g) salsa

2 cups (256 g) diced frozen hash browns, thawed

8 large eggs, beaten

2 tablespoons (28 ml) water

½ cup (120 ml) heavy cream

1¼ cups (320 g) salsa verde, divided

½ cup (8 g) chopped fresh cilantro, divided

8 flour tortillas (8 inches, or 20 cm)

2 cups (225 g) shredded cheddar cheese

¼ cup (45 g) diced tomatoes, for garnish

1 Preheat the oven to 375°F (190°C, or gas mark 5). Coat a 9- x 13-inch (23 x 33 cm) baking dish with nonstick cooking spray. Set aside.

2 In a large skillet, cook the ground venison and diced poblano peppers over medium-high heat until the venison is browned, about 5–6 minutes. Break the meat up with your spatula as it cooks. Drain any excess oil from the pan.

3 Add the salt, chili powder, cayenne, and black pepper to the venison. Pour salsa over the top. Mix well and then remove from the pan.

4 In the same pan, brown the frozen hash browns for just 2–3 minutes. They will not be cooked, just lightly toasted. Mix into the venison mixture.

5 Beat the eggs in a medium-sized bowl with 2 tablespoons (28 ml) of water. Add to the same skillet and cook until the eggs are scrambled. Mix the venison mixture back into the skillet and stir until mixed evenly.

6 Prepare the enchilada sauce by whisking together the heavy cream, 1 cup (256 g) of the salsa verde, and half of the cilantro. Set aside.

7 To assemble the enchiladas, pour the remaining salsa verde in the bottom of the baking dish. Then, fill each tortilla with about ½ cup (120 ml) of the venison and egg mixture. Sprinkle a small amount of cheddar cheese over the filling before rolling the tortilla tightly. Place the rolled tortilla into the prepared pan with the seam-side down. Repeat this process until the baking dish is full.

8 Pour the enchilada sauce evenly over the enchiladas and top with the remaining cheddar cheese.

9 Bake for 25 minutes or until golden and bubbly.

10 Garnish with diced tomatoes and chopped fresh cilantro and serve.

VENISON BRUNCH BURGER

Let's face it: not everyone is into classic breakfast plates. I know I have a couple of friends who always go for a burger or sandwich when we go out to brunch. I love this recipe because it's filling and fresh at the same time. To make it, you start out by taking ground venison and mixing it with pork breakfast sausage, which not only pumps up the flavor but provides some much-needed fat for the otherwise lean venison. The combo gets seasoned with salty and sweet flavors and then formed into patties. The signature patty is the star, but it's made even better with toppings like bacon, onion, avocado, and melty cheese. All of those flavors are held together on a toasted English muffin, though you can sub in a brioche bun or even go bunless, making this the centerpiece of a salad.

Yield: 6 burgers

½ pound (225 g) ground venison

½ pound (225 g) pork breakfast sausage

½ teaspoon fennel seeds

¼ teaspoon salt

¼ teaspoon black pepper

2 tablespoons (30 g) brown sugar

¼ cup (80 g) maple syrup

6 slices bacon, cooked

6 slices cheddar cheese

6 large eggs

6 English muffins

Vegetable or peanut oil, for sautéing

Butter, for English muffins

1 In a large bowl, combine ground venison, pork sausage, fennel, salt, pepper, brown sugar, and maple syrup. Mix just until all ingredients are equally distributed.

2 Divide and form the ground meat mixture into six equal patties.

3 Cook the bacon in a large skillet over medium-high heat. Remove from the pan and place in the oven to keep warm. Discard the bacon grease.

4 Heat a drizzle of oil in the same skillet over medium-high heat and add three burgers. Allow to fry for 5 minutes and then flip. Cook for another 5 minutes until they reach an internal temperature of 165°F (74°C) and then top with a slice of cheddar cheese. Repeat this process with remaining three burgers. Place in a warm oven as they finish cooking.

5 Fry the eggs in the same skillet until over easy or to your desired doneness.

6 Toast both sides of the English muffins either in the same pan or in a toaster. Apply a small slather of butter to each.

7 Assemble the burgers. Place a venison patty onto the bottom half of each English muffin. Top with a cooked egg, a slice of bacon, and the top half of the English muffin.

ADDING FAT TO WILD GAME

Wild game tastes great but as a rule tends to be leaner than store-bought meats. I find adding a touch of fat can take many dishes to a whole new level. In some recipes, you may want to add a small amount of a very fatty and flavorful meat, like bacon. Or really go for it: wrapping wild game with thick slices of bacon is a great way to augment otherwise lean meats and add a ton of fat and flavor to a dish.

In other cases, I recommend blending something like ground beef in with ground venison so that fat can act as the emulsifying agent—helping the mixture to stick together and retain juiciness. It not only makes the dish more approachable for those not quite used to the flavors of wild game, but it helps improve the texture of the resulting dish (something even the most seasoned hunters and wild-game fanatics can appreciate).

COUNTRY-STYLE BISCUITS WITH VENISON GRAVY

Biscuits and gravy are something I could eat every weekend . . . maybe even every day. It's always the season for it if you ask me. While I have a few different recipes, this one focuses on making the most delicious gravy and keeps the biscuits easy. But if you want to make the biscuits from scratch, just see my recipe below. If there's deer sausage in the freezer at home, for an even quicker version, substitute that for the ground venison and simply omit the flavorings for the meat.

Yield: 4 servings, 2 biscuits and a ¼ of the gravy per serving

VENISON GRAVY

1 pound (455 g) ground venison

1 small onion, diced

4 garlic cloves, minced

1 teaspoon dried parsley

1 teaspoon dried sage

½ teaspoon crushed red pepper

⅛ teaspoon ground nutmeg

½ teaspoon fennel seeds, crushed

1 teaspoon Worcestershire sauce

3 tablespoons (42 g) butter

3 tablespoons (24 g) all-purpose flour

2 cups (475 ml) whole milk

1 teaspoon salt

½ teaspoon black pepper

BISCUITS

2 cups (240 g) baking mix (I use Bisquick.)

¼ cup (60 ml) melted butter

1 teaspoon salt

1 tablespoon (13 g) sugar

1 cup (235 ml) whole milk

MAKE THE BISCUITS

1   Preheat the oven to 375°F (190°C, or gas mark 5).

2   Mix the baking mix, melted butter, salt, and sugar together in a large bowl. Slowly add the milk. You may need more or less than 1 cup (235 ml). Use only enough so that the batter just holds together. Drop 8 large spoonfuls of batter, at least 2 inches (5 cm) apart, onto a baking sheet coated with nonstick cooking spray. Bake until browned, about 15–20 minutes. Set aside.

MAKE THE VENISON GRAVY

1   Cook the ground venison in a large skillet over medium-high heat, approximately 8 minutes. About halfway, before the venison is fully browned, add the onion, garlic, parsley, sage, crushed red pepper, nutmeg, fennel seeds, and Worcestershire sauce. Mix well. Break up the meat into crumbles with a spatula as it cooks.

2   Add the butter. Once the butter is melted, sprinkle the flour over top. Mix until you no longer see white.

3   Add 1 cup (235 ml) of milk. Stir and simmer. Slowly add the additional cup (235 ml) of milk and bring to a simmer. If it's too thick, gradually add more milk until the gravy is the right consistency.

4   Season with salt and pepper and serve over the biscuits.

VENISON BREAKFAST SKILLET

This one-pot breakfast is a perfect family meal. You start by browning and seasoning venison in a large skillet or Dutch oven and then add the hash browns, onions, and bell peppers. Once the potatoes are browned and the venison is cooked, you create a well for the eggs to cook in. Then, of course, add cheese! Thanks to a little planning, what could have been a three- or four-pan affair is ready to eat with just the one pan to clean afterward. If you already have venison breakfast sausage, feel free to swap that in and skip the seasonings for the venison for an even easier meal!

Yield: 6 servings

2 tablespoons (28 g) butter

1 pound (455 g) ground venison

1 teaspoon onion powder

1 teaspoon smoked paprika

½ teaspoon dried sage

½ teaspoon crushed red pepper

1 cup (125 g) refrigerated shredded hash browns

½ white onion, diced

½ green bell pepper, seeded and diced

6 large eggs, beaten

½ teaspoon salt

¼ teaspoon black pepper

½ cup (58 g) shredded cheddar cheese

1 teaspoon chopped green onions, for garnish

1 In a deep 12-inch (30 cm) cast-iron skillet or other heavy skillet, melt the butter. Add the ground venison. Cook over medium heat for 5 minutes. The venison should start to brown. Add the onion powder, paprika, sage, and crushed red pepper. Mix until the seasonings are evenly distributed.

2 Add the hash browns, onion, and bell pepper to the skillet. Cook until the potatoes are lightly browned, 15–20 minutes, stirring often.

3 Push the potato mixture to the sides of pan. Pour the eggs into the center of pan. Cook and stir the eggs over medium heat until they are completely set. Season with salt and pepper. Reduce the heat and stir to combine everything. Top with cheddar cheese. Cover and cook until the cheese is melted, 1–2 minutes.

4 Garnish with chopped green onion if desired and serve.

HONEY BUTTER PHEASANT BISCUIT

Yes, this dish is inspired by the famous chicken and biscuit sandwich, which is one of my all-time breakfast favorites. How do you improve such a classic? Well, I thought of three ways. First, sub in crispy fried pheasant. Second, make the biscuits from scratch. And third, there's a smear of honey butter that melts right on top of the sandwich. Going with a southern tradition, the pheasant in this recipe is marinated in buttermilk, with a touch of garlic salt, parsley, paprika, and parsley. These biscuits are from scratch, but still a pretty simple drop and bake recipe. If you want more of a shortcut recipe though, just see page 21.

Yield: 4 servings

4 boneless, skinless pheasant breasts, approximately 4–5 ounces (115 to 140 g) each, tenderized to equal widths

MARINADE

1 cup (235 ml) buttermilk

1 teaspoon garlic salt with parsley

½ teaspoon black pepper

½ teaspoon paprika

BISCUITS

2 cups (250 g) all-purpose flour

1 tablespoon (14 g) baking powder

½ teaspoon salt

1 tablespoon (13 g) granulated sugar

1 stick (½ cup, or 112 g) cold unsalted butter

¾ cup (175 ml) buttermilk

2 tablespoons (28 ml) melted butter, for tops of biscuits

HONEY BUTTER

2 tablespoons (40 g) honey

1 stick (½ cup, or 112 g) butter, softened

MARINATE THE PHEASANT

1 Tenderize the pheasant breasts to approximately ¼ inch (6 mm). (Note: if the pheasant breasts are too big to fit into the sandwich, cut in half.)

2 Place into an airtight container with a lid or a resealable plastic bag.

3 Combine the marinade ingredients into a medium-sized bowl. Stir until evenly mixed and pour over the pheasant breasts. Marinate overnight or for at least 2 hours in the refrigerator.

MAKE THE BISCUITS AND HONEY BUTTER

1 In a large bowl, whisk the flour, baking powder, salt, and sugar together until fluffy.

2 Using a box grater, grate the cold butter into the flour mixture and crumble with your hands.

3 Make a well in the middle of the flour and pour in the buttermilk. Gently mix until the ingredients are just moistened.

4 Pat into round balls and place into a greased baking dish (or a pie plate with the biscuits touching).

5 Bake at 450°F (230°C, or gas mark 8) for 15 minutes until golden brown. Brush the tops of biscuits with melted butter.

6 While the biscuits are cooking, prepare the honey butter. In a small bowl, mix together the honey and softened butter, cover, and store in the refrigerator until ready to use.

(Continued on next page)

(Continued from previous page)

. . . .

DREDGE

1 cup (125 g) all-purpose flour

2 tablespoons (16 g) cornstarch

1 teaspoon garlic salt with parsley

1 teaspoon black pepper

½ teaspoon cayenne pepper

1 cup (235 ml) vegetable or peanut oil, for frying

MAKE THE FRIED PHEASANT BREASTS

1 Mix the all-purpose flour, cornstarch, garlic salt with parsley, black pepper, and cayenne in a large bowl.

2 Take the pheasant out of the marinade and place into the batter mix. Cover the pheasant completely and pat into every crevice.

3 Heat the oil to 350°F (180°C). Fry the pheasant in the heated oil for 3 minutes. Flip and cook for another 3 minutes or until golden brown and cooked through.

4 Assemble your biscuit. Cut a biscuit in half. Place a pheasant breast on the bottom half of the biscuit and top with the honey butter and the biscuit top.

MY HUNTING DOGS

LAB (L.K.)

Labrador retrievers are one of the most versatile breeds on earth, hence why they are so popular with outdoorsmen. My lab was born and bred to track wounded deer, but when I took her in, her life became all about waterfowl and upland hunting. Sitting in a blind, watching the world come up with my dog on my right-hand side, both of us just as anxious as the other for the birds to start trickling in—it doesn't get much better. And it's a feeling only a handler and their dog would understand. She's always down to sit in the cold and rain with me. I couldn't ask for a better hunting companion. I've seen her retrieve many species over the years, but nothing beats her carrying around a big, fat late-season goose!

BEAGLES (REMINGTON AND BERETTA)

I grew up with a hunting beagle that was, let's say, not that much of a hunting dog. I never knew then that I would fall so in love with the breed and what they are capable of. I picked up my own two beagles years ago and named them Remington and Beretta. They were so small, only 5 pounds (2.3 kg). (What was I thinking about getting two puppies at one time? I certainly had my hands full!) A lot of time and effort was spent getting them used to running in the thick woods through briars, getting accustomed to gunshots, and chasing rabbits. After a few months of training, we went out on our first real hunt. After we got that first rabbit together, it was game on ever since.

As the years progress, I love watching them grow as hunters. They pick up new skills and improve every season. Some days we end up with fifteen rabbits and some days we end up with none. No matter, these dogs love hunting rabbits just as I do. There are never any complaints on their end. They are just as happy as me to be out there enjoying the chase. Honestly, sometimes I enjoy taking them out with no gun, just to watch them run rabbits and do what they love.

CHORIZO-INSPIRED WILD HOG EGG BITES

This recipe is hearty and filling with a touch of heat from the chorizo-like flavors. It is a delicious option for breakfast on the go that I think we could all appreciate! In this recipe, it's the ancho chili powder, paprika, oregano, and garlic that provide those chorizo flavors. To that, you'll add one pound (455 g) of any game meat. I chose wild hog because I think pork and the flavors of chorizo just belong together. Once you've got your meat flavored and ready to go, the rest is so simple—just combining meat, eggs, and cheese before baking. You'll be good to go in no time!

Yield: 24 egg bites

1 tablespoon (15 ml) extra-virgin olive oil

1 pound (455 g) ground wild hog

½ cup (75 g) green bell pepper, seeded and diced

2 tablespoons (16 g) ancho chili powder

1 tablespoon (7 g) smoked paprika

1 teaspoon dried oregano

½ teaspoon garlic powder

1 teaspoon salt, divided

12 large eggs

¼ cup (60 ml) half-and-half

½ teaspoon black pepper

8 ounces (225 g) shredded Mexican-style cheese blend

Finely chopped scallions, for garnish

1 Preheat the oven to 350°F (180°C, or gas mark 4).

2 Start by heating the olive oil in a nonstick skillet. Once the oil is hot, add the ground wild hog and bell pepper. Break up the meat as you sauté. Cook until the meat is just browned, about 8 minutes. Remove from the heat and then season with ancho chili powder, paprika, oregano, garlic powder, and ½ teaspoon salt.

3 In a medium-sized bowl, whisk the eggs with the half-and-half. Add ½ teaspoon each of salt and pepper.

4 Coat a 24-mini-muffin tin with nonstick cooking spray and fill each halfway with egg mixture.

5 Once they are all filled, add 1 tablespoon (15 ml) of the venison chorizo mixture to each one until you have used it all up. Top each with the Mexican style cheese.

6 Bake for about 12–15 minutes until the eggs are set and the edges are crisp.

7 Garnish with chopped scallions and serve.

APPETIZERS AND TAILGATE FOOD

Pheasant Fritters with Aioli 35

Venison, Bacon, and Swiss Dip............................. 37

Triple Wild Game Meatballs with Sweet Chili Sauce ... 39

California-Style Wild Turkey Sliders 43

Wild Turkey, Tomato, and Mozzarella Flatbread 45

Venison Taco Wonton Cups................................. 47

Venison Cheeseburger Mini Muffins 49

Sweet Heat BBQ Wild Turkey Bites................................. 51

Venison Cheeseburger Egg Rolls with Special Sauce.... 53

Spinach and Mushroom Venison Pinwheels.................. 55

Pretzel-Crusted Wild Turkey with Honey Mustard..... 57

Wild Hog Queso Verde 59

Rabbit Satay with Peanut Sauce... 61

PHEASANT FRITTERS WITH AIOLI

These fritters are perfectly crispy on the outside and at their best when packed full of sweet summer corn. Since they're only lightly fried until cooked through, the insides remain very fluffy. The garlic aioli elevates the dish and makes for a truly mouth-watering appetizer.

Yield: 12 fritters

FRITTERS

1 boneless, skinless pheasant breast, approximately 4–5 ounces (115 to 140 g)

½ teaspoon salt, divided

1 tablespoon (15 ml) extra-virgin olive oil

1 cup (154 g) fresh corn kernels

1 cup (125 g) all-purpose flour, plus more if needed

1 teaspoon baking powder

¼ teaspoon paprika

¼ teaspoon black pepper

1 can (14.75 ounces, or 418 g) creamed corn

2 large eggs, beaten

½ cup (58 g) shredded Monterey Jack cheese

½ cup (58 g) shredded cheddar cheese

¼ cup (4 g) finely chopped fresh cilantro

¼ cup (25 g) finely chopped green onion, white and green parts

Vegetable or peanut oil, for frying

AOILI

⅓ cup (75 g) mayonnaise

1 tablespoon (10 g) minced garlic

½ tablespoon freshly squeezed lemon juice

¼ teaspoon salt

¼ teaspoon black pepper

1   Preheat the oven to 400°F (200°C, or gas mark 6). Season the pheasant breast with ¼ teaspoon salt and then drizzle with olive oil. Bake for 18 minutes, flipping halfway, or until the internal temperature reaches 165°F (74°C). Finely dice the pheasant into small pieces.

2   Combine the pheasant, corn kernels, flour, baking powder, paprika, pepper, and remaining salt in a large mixing bowl. Stir until combined.

3   Add the creamed corn and beaten eggs. Stir until a thick batter forms and the ingredients are evenly distributed.

4   Add the Monterey Jack cheese, cheddar cheese, cilantro, and green onion. Gently stir until the ingredients are evenly combined. Set aside.

5   Before frying up the fritters, make the aioli so the flavors have time to meld. In a medium-sized bowl, combine the mayonnaise, garlic, lemon juice, and salt and pepper. Mix well and store in the refrigerator until ready to serve.

6   In a deep pan over medium-high heat, heat ½ inch (5 cm) of oil. Place two 1 tablespoon (15 ml)-sized mounds of the fritter mixture in the pan and then use a spatula to flatten them.

7   Cook the fritters for 3 minutes per side. They should look golden brown and crispy. Repeat the process with any remaining batter.

8   Serve warm with the aioli on the side for dipping.

VENISON, BACON, AND SWISS DIP

My mother used to make this dish for every party, though she used ground beef in hers. Of course, my own rendition of this recipe makes venison the star. Since the meat has a stronger flavor, I needed to add a touch of spice to bring it all together. Give it a try, and it just might become your go-to party or game-day dip as well. Serve with vegetables, breads, and crackers for dipping.

Yield: 4–6 servings

½ pound (225 g) ground venison

5 slices center-cut bacon, chopped

8 ounces (225 g) cream cheese, softened

½ cup (115 g) mayonnaise

2 teaspoons Dijon mustard

1–2 jalapeños, seeded and diced

1½ cups (165 g) shredded Swiss cheese

2 scallions, chopped

1 Preheat the oven to 400°F (200°C, or gas mark 6).

2 Brown the ground venison and bacon in a nonstick skillet over medium-high heat. Transfer the meat from the pan to a paper towel–lined plate and use a paper towel to remove some of the grease.

3 In a mixing bowl, combine the softened cream cheese, mayonnaise, Dijon mustard, diced jalapeño, Swiss cheese, and scallions with the cooked venison and bacon.

4 Place into a shallow 11- x 7-inch (28 x 18 cm) baking dish and bake until golden and bubbly at the edges, about 15–18 minutes.

5 Remove from the oven and place on a trivet or other heatproof surface so everyone can dip away while it's still hot.

TRIPLE WILD GAME MEATBALLS WITH SWEET CHILI SAUCE

This dish is truly a conversation starter. Wild hog carries a strong, nutty, rich flavor that is unique and perfectly complements the milder flavors of bear and venison. As if a bite of bear isn't enough of a conversation starter, this sweet, tangy dish also has a secret ingredient most people would never guess—grape jelly.

Yield: About 48 meatballs

MEATBALLS

1 pound (455 g) ground venison

½ pound (225 g) ground bear

½ pound (225 g) ground wild hog

2 large eggs, lightly beaten

½ cup (60 g) bread crumbs

1 tablespoon (15 ml) Worcestershire sauce

2 garlic cloves, minced

½ onion, thinly diced

½ teaspoon salt

¼ teaspoon black pepper

2 tablespoons (28 ml) vegetable or peanut oil, for frying

SAUCE

1½ cups (415 g) chili sauce

1 cup (340 g) grape jelly

2 tablespoons (30 g) brown sugar

3 teaspoons (15 g) Dijon mustard

2 tablespoons (12 g) sliced green onions, for garnish

MAKE THE MEATBALLS

1 In a large bowl, combine the ground venison, bear, and wild hog; eggs; bread crumbs; Worcestershire sauce; garlic; onion; salt; and pepper.

2 Use your hands to mix the meatball mixture until well blended but avoid overmixing.

3 Shape the mixture into 1-inch (2.5 cm) balls (you should have around 48 total).

COOK THE MEATBALLS

1 Heat the oil in a large skillet over medium heat. Add the meatballs to the skillet and brown in the pan for 10-15 minutes, rotating on all sides. Drain on paper towels.

2 Add the chili sauce, grape jelly, brown sugar, and Dijon mustard to the slow cooker. Stir the sauce together using a spoon until evenly mixed.

3 Add the browned meatballs to the slow cooker.

4 Cook on high for 2–3 hours or low for 3–4 hours. Turn the slow cooker to warm until ready to serve.

5 Garnish with sliced green onion prior to serving.

Some amount of game flavor is to be expected, and honestly, it's part of the intended experience when eating wild game! That said, there are things you can do to reduce the amount of what for lack of a better term I'd call *overly gamey* flavor. Overcoming this potential pitfall starts in the field. Proper handling, including timely and precise field dressing, can prevent many flavor problems. Once you begin the butchering process, it is important to remove all the silver skin and visible fat. Deer fat is not as tasty as most other meats. It actually adds to the gaminess.

If you simply don't feel like you can get used to the taste of wild game or the flavor of fully rutted buck, start with blended ground meat. I'd recommend starting out at a 60 to 40 percent ratio of your game meat to pork. Snack sticks and sausages are another great way to experience wild game.

Unwanted toughness is another common complaint for those new to wild game. For larger cuts, I recommend cooking low and slow in a moist environment. Smoking, making stews, and braising dishes are great options that build flavor while helping your meat come out perfectly tender.

Brining is a centuries-old method of using salt, water, and at times other spices to infuse flavor in wild and domestic meats. Wild game meats can be brined to help remove unwanted flavors and make the meat more tender at the same time.

Last but not least, marinades are a classic way to add flavor to steaks—and that is true when it comes to wild game as well. Your marinade should include an acid to help break down meat fibers, an oil to add moisture, and spices to create flavor (see page 164 for a few of my favorites).

CALIFORNIA-STYLE WILD TURKEY SLIDERS

These sliders are a cute, fun dish for any party! The sweetness of the rolls complements the freshness of the avocado and tomato. The melted mozzarella over top of the perfectly cooked turkey breast is to die for. Tip: To save yourself time when you're hosting, make the turkey the night before and store in the refrigerator.

Yield: 3–4 servings

1 boneless, skinless wild turkey breast, approximately 2 pounds (900 g)

½ teaspoon kosher salt

½ teaspoon black pepper

¼ cup (15 g) minced fresh parsley

¼ cup (10 g) minced fresh basil

2 garlic cloves, minced

1 tablespoon (15 ml) Worcestershire sauce

1 package Hawaiian sweet rolls (12 count)

¼ cup (60 g) mayonnaise

1 pound (455 g) sliced mozzarella cheese

½ red onion, sliced thin

2 Roma tomatoes, sliced thin

4–6 strips bacon, cooked and chopped

2 ripe avocados, sliced

3 tablespoons (42 g) butter, melted

1 Place the wild turkey breast in the bottom of a slow cooker. Add the salt, pepper, parsley, basil, garlic, and Worcestershire sauce over top of the turkey. Cook on low for 8 hours or on high for 4 hours. Shred the breast with two forks.

2 Preheat the oven to 350°F (180°C, or gas mark 4).

3 Split the rolls in half horizontally and place the bottom halves on a greased 9- x 13-inch (23 x 33 cm) baking sheet. Spread mayonnaise evenly onto the bottom layer of the slider buns. Top with the shredded turkey and then the mozzarella cheese.

4 Layer the red onion, tomato, bacon, and avocado. Close the sandwiches with the top bun.

5 Brush melted butter over the top of the sliders.

6 Bake for 10–12 minutes. The buns should be golden, and the cheese should be melted.

7 Remove from the oven and serve immediately.

WILD TURKEY, TOMATO, AND MOZZARELLA FLATBREAD

For me, tomato and mozzarella are a match made in heaven. Picture fresh tomatoes and mozzarella combined with shredded, seasoned wild turkey sitting atop a crispy, garlicky grilled naan bread that's hot off the grill and then topped with fresh basil and arugula—that's a recipe for pure joy. Once you try it, you'll definitely be coming back for seconds!

Yield: 4 servings

½ boneless, skinless wild turkey breast, approximately 1 pound (455 g)

2 tablespoons (28 ml) extra-virgin olive oil, divided

1 tablespoon (6 g) Italian seasoning

2 naan breads

3 garlic cloves, minced

8 ounces (225 g) fresh mozzarella cheese, thinly sliced

1 cup (150 g) cherry tomatoes, quartered

6 basil leaves, julienned

½ cup (10 g) loosely packed arugula

¼ teaspoon salt

¼ teaspoon black pepper

1 Preheat the grill to medium-high heat.

2 Cut the wild turkey breast into equal pieces for grilling. Drizzle with 1 tablespoon (15 ml) of olive oil and season with Italian seasoning. Place on the grill and cook for 6 minutes per side or until temperature reaches 165°F (74°C). Once cooked, set on a plate and shred with two forks.

3 Brush the remaining tablespoon (15 ml) of olive oil over both pieces of naan and then brush with the garlic. Top with the fresh mozzarella cheese, tomatoes, and shredded wild turkey.

4 Place directly on the grill and cook for 8–10 minutes with the lid closed. The cheese should be melted, and the naan should be golden brown.

5 Remove from the grill; top with fresh basil, arugula, salt, and pepper; and serve.

VENISON TACO WONTON CUPS

These are bite-sized perfection! It will be hard for your guests to eat just one, as you get all of the wonderful flavors of tacos in every bite. The wontons provide the perfect crunch around the warm taco-flavored venison. The toppings add freshness to the dish that ties it all together. This recipe has minimal preparation time and cooking time, making it an easy recipe for any last-minute gathering.

Yield: 4 servings

2 tablespoons (28 ml) extra-virgin olive oil

1 pound (455 g) ground venison

½ onion, diced

1 package (1 ounce, or 28 g) taco seasoning mix

24 wonton wrappers

8 ounces (225 g) shredded cheddar cheese

½ cup (115 g) sour cream

4 Roma tomatoes, diced

2 green onions, sliced

1 Preheat the oven to 400°F (200°C, or gas mark 6).

2 Add the olive oil to a large skillet over medium heat. Add the ground venison and onion and cook for 6–8 minutes or until the venison is no longer pink. Break up the meat as it cooks.

3 Stir in the taco seasoning and remove from the heat.

4 Coat a 12-cup muffin tin with nonstick cooking spray. Place one of the wonton wrappers into each of the wells.

5 Spoon 1 tablespoon (15 ml) of the venison and onion mixture onto each wrapper. Sprinkle approximately 2 tablespoons (28 ml) of cheddar cheese on top.

6 Create a second layer by placing a second wonton layer on top of each well, pressing it onto the bottom layer. Then, repeat the process of topping with the venison and onion mixture and then cheddar cheese in all of the wonton cups.

7 Bake for 10–15 minutes. The cheese should be brown, and the edges should be brown.

8 Top each wonton cup with a small dollop of sour cream, sprinkle the diced tomatoes and sliced green onions over each, and serve.

VENISON CHEESEBURGER MINI MUFFINS

Venison burgers are a popular dish with hunters and their families. While it may take the uninitiated some getting used to, there's no arguing that venison burgers provide a rich and earthy taste compared with commercial beef. If you have a friend or family member who's not ready for the full-on burger though, try this appetizer. It provides all the flavors you get from a venison burger in a moist and fluffy muffin—so there's a higher ratio of other flavors to meat!

Yield: 24 mini muffins

1 pound (455 g) ground venison

¼ teaspoon salt

¼ teaspoon black pepper

½ teaspoon garlic powder

½ teaspoon onion powder

1 tablespoon (15 ml) Worcestershire sauce

1 cup (115 g) shredded cheddar cheese

½ cup (120 ml) whole milk

2 large eggs

¼ cup (60 g) ketchup, plus more for serving

1 teaspoon mustard, plus more for serving

½ cup (54 g) pancake mix

1 Preheat the oven to 425°F (220°C, or gas mark 7).

2 In a large skillet, brown the ground venison over medium-high heat for approximately 6 minutes. Drain and set aside to cool for 5 minutes.

3 Once the venison has cooled, stir in the salt, pepper, garlic powder, onion powder, Worcestershire sauce, and cheddar cheese.

4 In a medium-sized bowl, stir the milk, eggs, ketchup, mustard, and pancake mix with a whisk until blended. Fold in the venison and cheese mixture.

5 Coat a mini muffin tin with nonstick cooking spray. Spoon the batter into the wells, pressing down with the back of the spoon as you go.

6 Bake for 15–18 minutes or until the toothpick comes out clean. The muffins should be golden brown. Let cool for 5 minutes.

7 Use a thin knife to loosen the muffins from the pan. Serve with additional ketchup and mustard for dipping.

SWEET HEAT BBQ WILD TURKEY BITES

Finger food just got a whole lot better. In this dish, wild turkey is seasoned to perfection with flavors of garlic and chili. They are then wrapped in a thin piece of bacon and smothered in a spicy and sweet sauce that has a hint of garlic flavor to it as well.

Yield: 8 servings

1 boneless, skinless wild turkey breast, approximately 2 pounds (900 g), cut into 1-inch (2.5 cm) pieces

1 tablespoon (8 g) chili powder

1 teaspoon paprika

1 teaspoon cayenne pepper

½ teaspoon garlic salt

½ teaspoon black pepper

1 tablespoon (9 g) loosely packed light brown sugar

1 package (12 ounces, or 340 g) center-cut bacon, cut in half

Sliced green onions, for garnish

Ranch dressing, for dipping

SWEET HEAT SAUCE

½ cup (125 g) sweet barbecue sauce (I use Sweet Baby Ray's.)

2 tablespoons (28 ml) buffalo sauce (I use Frank's Red Hot Buffalo.)

1 tablespoon (10 g) minced garlic

1 Preheat the oven to 400°F (200°C, or gas mark 6).

2 Line a large baking sheet with parchment paper.

3 Place the cut turkey pieces into a medium-sized bowl. Sprinkle the chili powder, paprika, cayenne, garlic salt, black pepper, and brown sugar over top.

4 Wrap half a slice of bacon around each of the seasoned turkey pieces. Secure with a toothpick and then place on the parchment paper.

5 Place the baking sheet into the oven and bake for 25 minutes. While the turkey bites are cooking, combine the barbecue sauce, buffalo sauce, and garlic in a small bowl. Brush the sauce onto the turkey bites halfway through cooking.

6 Brush with another layer of sauce 5 minutes before the cook time is over. Bake until the temperature of the turkey has reached at least 165°F (74°C).

7 Garnish with sliced green onions and serve with ranch dressing for dipping.

VENISON CHEESEBURGER EGG ROLLS WITH SPECIAL SAUCE

There's a certain fast-food chain with golden arches that makes a signature double-stacked burger. When you bite into this crispy egg roll, you get all of the flavors of that burger, complete with the sauce, tucked inside an egg roll. I love how the melted cheese, pickles, onion, and notes of garlic are pulled together by the delicious ground venison. The sauce needs no introduction: it is wonderfully creamy, sweet, and tangy. I love to serve these as appetizers, but they make a great centerpiece for a family dinner too!

Yield: Makes about 12 egg rolls (6 servings)

1 pound (455 g) ground venison

2 teaspoons minced garlic

2 teaspoons Worcestershire sauce

1 tablespoon (7 g) onion powder

1 teaspoon paprika

½ teaspoon salt

½ teaspoon black pepper

12 egg roll wrappers

12 slices cheddar cheese

½ cup (72 g) dill pickles, diced

½ cup (80 g) red onion, diced

Bowl of water

Nonstick cooking spray

SPECIAL SAUCE

½ cup (115 g) mayonnaise

2 tablespoons (22 g) yellow mustard

2 tablespoons (30 g) ketchup

1 tablespoon (15 ml) apple cider vinegar

1   In a small bowl, combine all ingredients for the dipping sauce and stir until evenly mixed. Cover and place in the refrigerator until ready to serve.

2   In a skillet over medium heat, cook the ground venison for 8–10 minutes or until the meat is browned and no longer contains any pink.

3   Add the garlic into the pan and cook for an additional minute. Remove from the heat and drain any excess liquid.

4   Add the Worcestershire sauce, onion powder, paprika, and salt and pepper to the skillet. Mix well and then remove the pan from the burner.

5   Place an egg roll wrapper on a clean surface in a diamond shape. Place a slice of cheddar cheese in the center. Top with approximately 2 tablespoons (28 ml) of cooked venison and a pinch of diced pickles and red onion on top. Fold up the bottom half and tightly fold in the sides. Gently roll and then dip your fingertips in water and run around edges to dampen and seal.

6   Spray the air fryer and egg rolls with nonstick cooking spray and air-fry at 390°F (200°C) for 3 minutes each side or panfry in a skillet with oil for 1–2 minutes on each side.

7   Serve with the dipping sauce.

SPINACH AND MUSHROOM VENISON PINWHEELS

This is a quick and easy appetizer that is always a crowd pleaser. The puff pastry has a buttery taste with a slightly crunchy crust and a light and airy texture. It is filled with venison, mushrooms, and spinach that are married together with cream cheese.

Yield: Makes about 12 pinwheels (6 servings)

½ pound (225 g) ground venison

1 package (8 ounces, or 225 g) baby bella mushrooms, chopped

1 cup (30 g) loosely packed spinach

1 teaspoon garlic salt

½ teaspoon black pepper

2 packages (8 ounces, or 225 g each) refrigerated crescent rolls

1 package (8 ounces, or 225 g) cream cheese, softened, divided

1 egg, beaten

1 tablespoon (4 g) chopped fresh parsley, for garnish

1   Line 2 baking sheets with parchment paper.

2   Heat a large skillet over medium-high heat. Cook and stir the ground venison in the hot skillet until browned and crumbly, about 10 minutes. Drain and discard any grease.

3   Add the mushrooms, spinach, garlic salt, and pepper and cook until the spinach is wilted, stirring often. Remove from the heat.

4   Spread the dough from one package of crescent rolls out onto a clean surface and pinch the perforations together to create a single sheet of dough. Carefully spread the cream cheese on top of the entire sheet, leaving a ½-inch (1.3 cm) margin around the edges.

5   Repeat for the second package of crescent rolls and second package of cream cheese.

6   Layer the venison filling evenly on top of both pastry sheets.

7   Roll up the pastry tightly, starting from the longer side. Cut each roll into 1-inch (5 cm) pinwheels.

8   Repeat this step with the second roll. Refrigerate the rolls for 1 hour.

9   Preheat the oven to 375°F (190°C, or gas mark 5).

10 Lay the pinwheels flat on the parchment. Brush with the egg wash. Bake in the preheated oven until the pinwheels are golden brown, 15–20 minutes.

11 Garnish with chopped fresh parsley and serve.

PRETZEL-CRUSTED WILD TURKEY WITH HONEY MUSTARD

Pretzels and mustard just go together—there are no ifs, ands, or buts about it! The combination of the salt and the crunch of the pretzel breading with the sweet and tangy marinade and dipping sauce makes for a total slam dunk!

Yield: 4 servings

1 large boneless, skinless wild turkey breast, approximately 2½–3 pounds (1.1 to 1.4 kg)

6 ounces (170 g) thin pretzel sticks

6 tablespoons (90 ml) vegetable or peanut oil, for frying

HONEY MUSTARD

1 cup (225 g) mayonnaise

½ cup (120 g) Dijon mustard

½ cup (160 g) honey

Juice of 1 lemon

½ teaspoon paprika

½ teaspoon garlic powder

1 teaspoon kosher salt

1 Lay the wild turkey out on a flat surface. Using a meat mallet, pound out the turkey to approximately ¼-inch (6 mm) thick. Cut into equal finger food–sized tenders. Pat dry with a paper towel and set aside.

2 In a large bowl, whisk together the mayonnaise, Dijon mustard, honey, lemon juice, paprika, garlic powder, and salt. Pour half of the honey mustard sauce into a shallow dish and reserve the rest in the refrigerator until ready to serve.

3 Put the pretzels in a food processor and pulse to crumb consistency, about 20 seconds. Transfer to another shallow dish.

4 Dredge each turkey tender into the honey mustard sauce, coating the entire tender. Then, coat with the pretzel crumbs, pressing gently so that the pretzel crumbs adhere.

5 Preheat 3 tablespoons (45 ml) of oil in a skillet over medium-high heat. Add half of the turkey tenders and cook until golden brown and cooked through, approximately 5 minutes per side. Transfer to a paper towel–lined plate.

6 Discard the oil, wipe the skillet clean with a paper towel, and repeat with the remaining oil and turkey tenders.

7 Serve with the reserved honey mustard sauce.

WILD HOG QUESO VERDE

This is not your typical queso dip! The salsa verde is the obvious star of this dish, but the wild hog gives the dish more flavor—and helps to hold your guests' hunger off until dinner is ready. The poblano pepper adds a peppery, slightly smoky flavor to the dish. The cilantro is optional but recommended unless there's someone in your group who really can't stand it.

Yield: 6 servings

1 tablespoon (15 ml) vegetable or peanut oil

1 pound (455 g) ground wild hog

1 poblano pepper, seeded and diced

½ large onion, diced

1 pound (455 g) shredded white cheddar cheese

3 ounces (85 g) shredded Asiago cheese

1 cup (235 ml) whole milk, divided

1 jar (16 ounces, or 455 g) salsa verde

¼ cup (41 g) roasted corn, for garnish

1 tablespoon (1 g) chopped fresh cilantro, for garnish

Tortilla chips, for serving

1 Heat the oil in a large pot over medium heat. Add the ground wild hog, the diced poblano pepper, and the onion and cook until the wild hog is no longer pink and the vegetables are tender. Drain off any fat and return to the heat.

2 Place the cheddar cheese, Asiago cheese, milk, and salsa verde into the pot with the wild hog and vegetables. Cook, stirring occasionally, until melted and smooth.

3 Serve immediately, topped with roasted corn and chopped fresh cilantro and with tortilla chips on the side for dipping.

WILD HOG VS. STORE-BOUGHT PORK

There are many differences between wild hog and store-bought pork. Most commercial-grade pork live their lives confined to a pen or field while wild hogs are free to roam wherever they please. A free-range animal that is always on the move and foraging on a wide variety of foods results in richer, more flavorful meat. Big on flavor and lower in fat, wild hog meat is often incredibly lean in comparison to commercial grade. There's never any chance of added steroids or antibiotics to this game meat either. Overall, I find it has a superior taste and texture to pork, and wild hog is a treat for the whole family.

RABBIT SATAY WITH PEANUT SAUCE

Don't let the unfamiliar name of this dish put you off. The term "satay" simply refers to a grilled meat dish famous throughout Southeast Asia. The peanut sauce is sweet with a touch of spice from the chili garlic sauce. Since it is easy for rabbit to dry out, watch the temperature of the meat carefully while cooking.

Yield: 8 servings

Saddle of 4 rabbits, boneless, cut into 8 pieces, approximately ½ pound (225 g) in total

8 metal or wooden skewers, for cooking

MARINADE

2 tablespoons (28 ml) low-sodium soy sauce

1 tablespoon (15 ml) fish sauce

2 garlic cloves, minced

1 can (5½ ounces, or 165 ml) coconut milk

½ teaspoon ground cumin

½ teaspoon minced fresh ginger

PEANUT SAUCE

Juice of ½ lime

1 teaspoon honey

1 tablespoon (15 ml) low-sodium soy sauce

1 teaspoon ground ginger

2 teaspoons chili garlic sauce

1 can (5½ ounces, or 165 ml) coconut milk

3 tablespoons (48 g) smooth peanut butter

1. If you're not using metal skewers, soak at least eight wooden skewers in water for half an hour. This will prevent them from burning when cooking.

2. Place the pieces of rabbit meat into a large bowl or resealable plastic bag. Mix the marinade ingredients together in a small bowl and add to the bag. Mix the marinade and rabbit together using your hands, massaging the marinade into the rabbit. Cover and place in the refrigerator for at least 30 minutes.

3. While you wait for the rabbit to marinate, make the peanut sauce by whisking together the lime juice, honey, soy sauce, ginger, chili garlic sauce, coconut milk, and peanut butter in a small bowl. Set aside on the counter or in the refrigerator until ready to serve.

4. Remove the skewers from the water and shake to remove excess water. Preheat the grill to medium-high heat and then thread the rabbit pieces onto the skewers.

5. Add the skewers to the grill and cook, turning occasionally, until the rabbit is completely cooked through, reaching an internal temperature of 165°F (74°C), about 10–15 minutes.

6. Remove the rabbit skewers from the grill and place on plates or a large serving platter alongside the dipping sauce.

3

SOUPS,
STEWS, AND
SLOW-COOKED
MEALS

Italian Pheasant Noodle Soup 67

Venison Stuffed Pepper Soup 69

Creamy Wild Turkey and Mushroom Soup 71

Venison Cabbage Roll Soup 73

Venison Cheeseburger Soup 75

Asian Wild Turkey and Pot Sticker Soup 77

Venison and Irish Stout Sunday Stew 79

Green Chile Venison Stew 81

Wild Hog and Cider Stew 83

Rabbit Bourguignon (Rabbit Stewed in Red Wine) 85

Braised French Onion Pheasant 87

Slow-Cooker Garlic-Sesame Venison and Broccoli 89

Slow Cooker Venison Barbacoa 91

Slow Cooker Wild Turkey and Stuffing 93

Smoked Canada Goose Pastrami 95

Lemon Caper Braised Rabbit 97

ITALIAN PHEASANT NOODLE SOUP

Pheasant noodle soup is the first recipe in this chapter because it's one of my all-time favorites. While my dish is far from a traditional noodle soup, it is rich, creamy, and comforting. It is packed full of delicious vegetables, tender pheasant meat, and egg noodles. Of course, if you make your own stock from pheasants or other fowl, feel free to use that in place of chicken broth.

Yield: 6–8 servings

PHEASANT

4 boneless, skinless pheasant breasts, approximately 4–5 ounces (115 to 140 g) each

1 teaspoon Italian seasoning

¼ teaspoon salt

Pinch of black pepper

1 tablespoon (15 ml) extra-virgin olive oil

SOUP

1½ tablespoons (25 ml) extra-virgin olive oil

1 large white onion, diced

3 carrots, peeled and chopped

3 stalks celery, diced

2 tablespoons (20 g) minced garlic

2 tablespoons (16 g) all-purpose flour

32 ounces (950 ml) chicken broth

1 container (16 ounces, or 455 g) heavy cream

1 can (10½ ounces, or 300 g) cream of chicken soup

¼ cup (15 g) chopped fresh parsley

2 tablespoons (8 g) dried thyme

1 package (12 ounces, or 340 g) wide egg noodles, cooked al dente

1 Preheat the oven to 350°F (180°C, or gas mark 4).

2 Pat the pheasant breasts dry with a paper towel. Combine the Italian seasoning, salt, and pepper in a small bowl. Season both sides with the seasoning mixture and then drizzle with olive oil.

3 Place into a casserole dish or onto a baking sheet and bake for 20–25 minutes, flipping halfway. Note: The cook time may vary depending on the size of your pheasants. The internal temperature should read 165°F (74°C) once fully cooked.

4 In a large pot, heat the olive oil over medium heat. Add the onion, carrot, and celery and sauté until tender, about 3–4 minutes. Then, add the garlic and sauté for 1 minute longer.

5 Sprinkle the flour over the vegetables. Cook, mixing constantly, for 1–2 minutes, until the flour coats the vegetables and turns a golden color.

6 Add the chicken broth, heavy cream, and cream of chicken soup into the pot. Bring to a boil, stirring the pot often.

7 Reduce the heat to simmer and then mix in the pheasant, parsley, and thyme. Taste the soup and add any salt or pepper if desired.

8 To serve, portion the cooked egg noodles into bowls and then pour the hot soup over top.

VENISON STUFFED PEPPER SOUP

Stuffed pepper soup has been a go-to hearty soup for me ever since the first time I tried it. It's an easy soup to make with simple ingredients: ground venison, rice, bell peppers, and onions in a tomato-based broth. The venison is rich in flavor but still a leaner red meat option, making this dish less heavy than a traditional stuffed pepper soup with beef. The flavors of the bell peppers and tomatoes are the superstars of the dish, but there's more going on under the surface—and of course, the rice is tender and helps fill you up. For me, this dish has to have some kick to it, but feel free to adjust the heat level to your taste.

Yield: 6–8 servings

2 tablespoons (28 ml) extra-virgin olive oil

1½ pounds (680 g) ground venison

½ teaspoon salt

¼ teaspoon black pepper

1 large onion, chopped

2 medium green bell peppers, seeded and chopped

1 medium red bell pepper, seeded and chopped

4 garlic cloves, minced

2 cans (14½ ounces, or 410 g each) diced fire roasted tomatoes

1 jar (15 ounces, or 425 g) tomato sauce

2 tablespoons (28 ml) hot sauce

2 cups (475 ml) beef broth

2 tablespoons (8 g) chopped fresh parsley, plus more for garnish

1 tablespoon (7 g) paprika

1 teaspoon dried basil

1 teaspoon dried oregano

½ teaspoon dried thyme

1 cup (186 g) cooked white rice

1 In a large pot over medium heat, heat 1 tablespoon (15 ml) of olive oil. Once hot, add the ground venison and season with salt and pepper. Cook, stirring occasionally while breaking up the venison, until browned. This should take 5–7 minutes. Once browned, drain any excess liquid and set aside.

2 In the same pot, heat the rest of the olive oil and then add the onion and bell peppers. Sauté the bell peppers and onions for about 3 minutes. They should still be fairly crisp at this point.

3 Add the garlic to the pot and sauté just until fragrant, approximately 30 seconds.

4 Pour in the canned tomatoes, tomato sauce, hot sauce, and beef broth. Then, add the parsley, paprika, basil, oregano, and thyme. Bring to a light boil, add the venison, and then reduce the heat to low. Cover and simmer for 30 minutes to allow for the flavors to combine and the bell peppers to become tender. Stir occasionally.

5 Stir in the cooked rice. Add any additional salt or pepper to the soup if desired.

6 Garnish with chopped fresh parsley and serve warm.

CREAMY WILD TURKEY AND MUSHROOM SOUP

Comforting, cozy, and creamy, this wild turkey and mushroom soup is full of flavor. It's loaded with big chunks of wild turkey meat, onions, carrots, celery, orzo, and of course, plenty of mushrooms. To make this dish, you start by cubing the wild turkey breast into 1-inch (2.5 cm) pieces. You then brown the wild turkey chunks until they get a golden crisp on the outside but are not fully cooked. I've found this is the key to ensuring flavorful, but still tender, turkey ever time.

Yield: 6–8 servings

1 large boneless, skinless wild turkey breast, approximately 2½–3 pounds (1.1 to 1.4 kg)

1 teaspoon salt

1 teaspoon black pepper

1 tablespoon (28 ml) extra-virgin olive oil

2 tablespoons (28 g) unsalted butter

1 large yellow onion, diced

3 large carrots, peeled and diced

2 stalks celery, diced

3 garlic cloves, minced

8 ounces (225 g) baby portobello mushrooms, thinly sliced

4 ounces (115 g) shiitake mushrooms, thinly sliced

½ teaspoon dried oregano

¼ teaspoon dried thyme

½ teaspoon dry mustard

2 tablespoons (16 g) all-purpose flour

3 cups (700 ml) chicken broth

2½ cups (570 ml) whole milk

¼ cup (28 g) dry orzo pasta

2 tablespoons (8 g) chopped fresh parsley, for garnish

Croutons, for garnish (optional)

1. Cut the wild turkey breast into 1-inch (2.5 cm) pieces. Pat the pieces dry with a paper towel and then season with salt and pepper.

2. In a large stockpot or Dutch oven, add the olive oil and set the burner to medium heat. Add the wild turkey pieces and cook for 10 minutes so that the turkey is just browned on the outside, but not fully cooked. Stir often. Remove the wild turkey from the pot with a slotted spoon and set aside.

3. Add the butter to the pot. Once melted, add the onion, carrots, and celery. Cook, stirring occasionally, until the vegetables begin to soften, about 5 minutes.

4. Stir in the garlic, mushrooms, oregano, thyme, and dry mustard. Cook for 8–10 minutes or until mushrooms are soft, continuing to stir occasionally.

5. Sprinkle the flour over the veggies and cook for about 1 minute, stirring constantly.

6. Stir in the chicken broth and milk and then bring to a simmer. Add the orzo and wild turkey pieces. Simmer, uncovered, for 10–15 minutes or until the pasta is tender, the turkey is cooked through, and the soup has thickened.

7. Garnish with chopped fresh parsley and croutons if desired and serve.

VENISON CABBAGE ROLL SOUP

Cabbage rolls are delicious, and I love making them with venison. But sometimes, you just don't have the time to make a recipe like that. Enter this soup, which gives you all the flavors of stuffed cabbage rolls with only a small portion of the active cooking time! The pork adds a slight sweetness and some fat to the otherwise lean venison, so I do recommend including it in this soup. The meats, together with the tender cabbage, rice, and tomato broth, are a sure win.

Yield: 8 servings

1 tablespoon (15 ml) extra-virgin olive oil

1 large onion, diced

1 pound (455 g) ground venison

½ pound (225 g) ground pork

1½ teaspoons paprika

1 teaspoon kosher salt

¼ teaspoon black pepper

3 garlic cloves, minced

4 cups (950 ml) beef broth

1 can (15 ounces, or 425 g) tomato sauce

1 can (14½ ounces, or 410 g) petite diced tomatoes, not drained

1 cup (235 ml) water

2 tablespoons (30 g) packed light brown sugar

1 tablespoon (15 ml) Worcestershire sauce

1 teaspoon apple cider vinegar

1 bay leaf

1 medium head cabbage, chopped and core removed

½ cup (93 g) uncooked long grain rice

¼ cup (15 g) chopped fresh parsley, for garnish

1 Heat 1 tablespoon (15 ml) of olive oil in a large pot or Dutch oven over medium-high heat until shimmering. Add the onion, ground venison, ground pork, and paprika. Season with 1 teaspoon kosher salt and ¼ teaspoon pepper. Cook, breaking up the meat into small pieces with a wooden spoon, until the meat is cooked through and the onion is softened, about 10 minutes.

2 Stir in the garlic, beef broth, tomato sauce, diced tomatoes, water, brown sugar, Worcestershire sauce, apple cider vinegar, and bay leaf. Stir to combine and then use the spoon to scrape any browned bits from the bottom of the pot. Increase the heat to high and bring to a boil.

3 Add the cabbage and rice to the pot. Reduce the heat to maintain a simmer and cook, stirring occasionally, until the rice and cabbage are tender, about 30 minutes.

4 Remove the bay leaf. Taste and season the soup with more salt and pepper as needed.

5 Garnish with chopped fresh parsley and serve.

VENISON CHEESEBURGER SOUP

This cheeseburger soup is a creamy combination of cheese, venison, bacon, vegetables, and potatoes and finished with your favorite burger toppings. It is a recipe that is sure to be a favorite in your family! I recommend using a block of high-quality cheddar cheese and grating it yourself to take this dish to the next level.

Yield: 8 servings

1 pound (455 g) ground venison

½ teaspoon garlic salt

¼ teaspoon black pepper

⅛ teaspoon paprika

6 slices bacon, chopped

2 tablespoons (28 g) unsalted butter

1 onion, finely diced

1 large carrot, peeled and grated

2 stalks celery, chopped

¼ cup (32 g) all-purpose flour

32 ounces (950 ml) chicken broth

4 small russet potatoes, peeled and diced

1 teaspoon dried basil

1 teaspoon dried parsley

2 cups (475 ml) whole milk

2 cups (225 g) shredded cheddar cheese

¼ cup (60 g) sour cream

OPTIONAL TOPPINGS

Diced tomato

Diced dill pickle

Shredded cheddar cheese

Chopped fresh parsley

1 Place a large pot or Dutch oven over medium heat. Begin to brown the ground venison, breaking it up with a spoon as it cooks. Season with garlic salt, pepper, and paprika. Cook until the venison is just browned, 5–6 minutes.

2 Remove the venison from the pot and set aside. Add the bacon to the pot and cook for 5–6 minutes or until crisp. Remove the bacon from the pot onto a plate. Chop and then set aside.

3 Drain most of the bacon grease, leaving a small amount in the bottom of the pot for flavor.

4 Return the pot to the heat and add the butter. Once the butter melts, add the onion, carrots, and celery. Cook for 3–4 minutes or until the vegetables start softening. Stir in the flour and cook for 1–2 minutes. Gradually add the chicken broth, scraping up any browned bits from the bottom of the pot.

5 Bring to a boil and then add the potatoes, basil, parsley, and browned venison and reduce to a simmer. Simmer for 15 minutes or until the potatoes are tender.

6 Add the milk and stir well. Add the cheddar cheese and most of the bacon pieces (but save a small portion of bacon for garnishing!). Cook for 3–4 minutes or until the cheese has melted.

7 Remove from the heat and stir in the sour cream. Garnish with your favorite toppings.

ASIAN WILD TURKEY AND POT STICKER SOUP

This pot sticker soup is packed with onions, carrots, bok choy, and wild turkey. As you sip the broth, you'll notice ginger and soy flavors that are out of this world. I also like that this soup is satisfying and filling without making you want to sit on the couch the rest of the night the way a rich, creamy soup might.

Yield: 6 servings

2 tablespoons (28 ml) sesame oil, divided

2 large carrots, peeled and julienned

3 green onions, thinly sliced with white and green parts separated

4 garlic cloves, minced

2 tablespoons (8 g) freshly grated ginger

1 small boneless, skinless wild turkey breast, approximately 1½ pounds (680 g), or half a larger breast

½ teaspoon salt

¼ teaspoon black pepper

5 cups (1.2 L) chicken stock

2 cups (475 ml) water

3 tablespoons (45 ml) low-sodium soy sauce

3 baby bok choy leaves, chopped (white parts discarded)

1 bag (1½ pounds, or 680 g) frozen pot stickers or dumplings

1 Heat 1 tablespoon (15 ml) of sesame oil in a large pot over medium heat. Add the carrots and sauté for 3 minutes. Add the white parts of the green onions, garlic, and ginger and sauté for 2 minutes longer. Remove from the pot and set aside.

2 Cut the wild turkey into three or four equal portions. Cover with plastic wrap and pound to an even thickness using the flat side of a meat mallet.

3 Season both sides of the wild turkey lightly with salt and pepper. Heat the rest of the sesame oil in the pot. Then add the wild turkey pieces and cook for 2 minutes per side until the wild turkey has a golden brown color on the outside.

4 Pour in the chicken stock, water, soy sauce, and vegetable mixture. Bring to a boil and then reduce heat to medium-low and simmer until turkey is cooked through. This should take 5–7 minutes once simmering.

5 Remove the turkey from the soup and transfer to a plate. Let rest for 3 minutes and then cut into strips or shred.

6 Meanwhile, stir in the bok choy and pot stickers and cook for 3–5 minutes. Stir the turkey back into the soup.

7 Serve warm, garnished with the green parts of the green onions.

VENISON AND IRISH STOUT SUNDAY STEW

As the name of this recipe suggests, this dish is inspired by everyone's favorite Irish beer. It's not just for a catchy recipe title though. As the stout cooks into the stew, the alcohol evaporates and leaves you with a deep and robust flavor—as well as a richer brown color. As you get past the flavors of the sauce, the venison is fall-apart tender and the vegetables pair perfectly with the venison in the sauce. The crisp pancetta gives an added saltiness and richness to the dish, but you can easily swap with bacon or even skip it if you prefer it without.

Yield: 6 servings

2 pound (900 g) venison roast, cut into 2-inch (5 cm) pieces

1 teaspoon kosher salt

1 teaspoon black pepper

2 tablespoons (28 g) butter

1 large yellow onion, roughly chopped

3 garlic cloves, minced

6 ounces (170 g) diced pancetta (or bacon)

1 cup (130 g) carrots, peeled and cut into ½-inch (1.3 cm) chunks

1 cup (100 g) roughly chopped celery

3 tablespoons (24 g) all-purpose flour

1 bottle (12 ounces, or 355 ml) Irish stout

3 cups (700 ml) beef broth

3 tablespoons (48 g) tomato paste

1 tablespoon (15 ml) Worcestershire sauce

2 bay leaves

3 sprigs fresh thyme

Chopped fresh parsley, for garnish

1 Cut the venison into 2-inch (5 cm) pieces. Pat dry with a paper towel and season with salt and pepper.

2 Add 2 tablespoons (28 g) of butter to a 5-quart (4.7 L) Dutch oven or a large pot on medium-high heat. Add the venison pieces and brown well on all sides, 6–8 minutes. Remove from the pan.

3 Lower the heat to medium and add the onion. Cook for 3 minutes until just softening and then add the garlic and pancetta. Cook until the pancetta is browned, approximately 5 minutes.

4 Add the carrots and celery and continue to cook for 3–5 minutes.

5 Sprinkle flour over the mixture and mix well for 1 minute. There should be a golden brown film over the vegetables.

6 Pour in the Irish stout, beef broth, tomato paste, and Worcestershire sauce. Mix well and add the bay leaves and thyme sprigs.

7 Return the venison to the pot (including any juices). Cover the pot and lower the heat to a very gentle simmer. Cook for 2 hours—the venison should tender. Remove the lid and then simmer for another 30–45 minutes or until the venison falls apart at a touch and the sauce has reduced and thickened slightly.

8 Remove the bay leaves and thyme. Garnish with chopped fresh parsley and serve with bread or over mashed potatoes.

GREEN CHILE VENISON STEW

This stew is absolutely loaded with Hatch green chiles, potatoes, spices, and chunks of tender venison. Just wait until you smell the aromatics: they will waft through your house long before you get to grab a bowl! This dish would be as equally delicious if you substituted the venison roast for a roast from a wild hog.

Yield: 8 servings

3 pound (1.4 kg) venison roast, cut into 1-inch (2.5 cm) cubes

¼ cup (32 g) all-purpose flour

1 teaspoon salt, divided

½ teaspoon black pepper

½ teaspoon garlic powder

2 tablespoons (28 ml) extra-virgin olive oil

1 large onion, roughly chopped

3 garlic cloves, peeled and diced

1 can (14 ounces, or 390 g) chopped green chiles, or 6 Hatch green chiles, roasted and chopped into ½-inch (1.3 cm) pieces

2 cups (475 ml) chicken broth

1 can (10 ounces, or 285 g) green enchilada sauce

1 tablespoon (7 g) ground cumin

1 tablespoon (3 g) dried Mexican oregano

1 pound (455 g) red new potatoes, cleaned and cut into ¾-inch (2 cm) pieces

Chopped fresh cilantro, for garnish

1 Combine the venison cubes, flour, ½ teaspoon salt, pepper, and garlic powder in a 1-gallon (3.8 L) resealable plastic bag. Shake to coat thoroughly.

2 In a large pot or Dutch oven, heat the olive oil over medium heat. Add the onion and garlic and sauté until just starting to become translucent, approximately 3 minutes.

3 Add the seasoned venison and cook until browned, approximately 5 minutes, stirring often to ensure all the sides are browned.

4 Add the green chiles, chicken broth, green enchilada sauce, cumin, Mexican oregano, and remaining ½ teaspoon of salt to the Dutch oven and bring to a boil. Reduce the heat to low, cover, and simmer for 45 minutes.

5 Add the potatoes and bring to a boil. Once it's boiling, reduce the heat to a simmer and cook until the potatoes are tender, 15–20 minutes.

6 Garnish with chopped fresh cilantro. Serve by itself, over rice, or with warm tortillas.

ROASTED GREEN CHILE RECIPE

Slice the green chile peppers in half lengthwise and set them onto a baking sheet.

Bake them at 400°F (200°C, or gas mark 6) for 20 minutes. The skins should be blistered, and the peppers should start to become tender.

WILD HOG AND CIDER STEW

This dish carries a savory flavor with a subtle tang. It has the perfect touch of sweetness from the apples and cider. People have been pairing apples with domestic pork for ages, so I knew apple would pair well with the nutty and rich flavors of wild hog. And just like cooking with beer, I find cooking with hard cider helps tenderize the meat and add a bit more complexity than if you just added something like sweet nonalcoholic cider. (Though of course, it's fine to make that swap if you prefer not to cook with spirits!)

Yield: 6 servings

1 tablespoon (15 ml) extra-virgin olive oil

3 slices thick-cut bacon, diced

2 pounds (900 g) wild hog shoulder, cut into 2-inch (5 cm) chunks

1 teaspoon kosher salt

½ teaspoon black pepper

3 medium shallots, diced

1 teaspoon dried thyme

½ teaspoon dried sage

2 bay leaves

1 bottle (12 ounces, or 355 ml) dry hard cider

2 tablespoons (28 ml) apple cider vinegar

2 tablespoons (30 g) Dijon mustard

1 tablespoon (15 g) horseradish

2 cups (475 ml) chicken broth

4 carrots, peeled and cut into ½-inch (1.3 cm) chunks

1 apple, peeled, cored, and cut into 1-inch (2.5 cm) pieces

2 stalks celery, chopped

Chopped fresh parsley, for garnish

1 Heat the olive oil in a large Dutch oven or heavy pot over medium-high heat. Cook the bacon until crisp and then transfer to a bowl and set aside.

2 Season the wild hog with salt and pepper on all sides. Add to the Dutch oven and brown in batches. Transfer to the bowl with bacon.

3 Reduce the heat to low and add the shallots. Cook, scraping browned bits from the bottom of the pot, until the shallots are golden, about 8 minutes. Add the reserved bacon and wild hog and then add the thyme, sage, and bay leaves.

4 Pour in the cider, apple cider vinegar, Dijon mustard, horseradish, and chicken broth and bring to boil. Once boiling, add the carrots, apple, and celery and reduce the heat to simmer and cover. Cook for 1 hour, stirring occasionally.

5 Remove the bay leaves. Garnish with chopped fresh parsley and serve over mashed potatoes or noodles.

RABBIT BOURGUIGNON (RABBIT STEWED IN RED WINE)

It sounds fancy, but Bourguignon simply means cooked in red wine. Traditionally, this dish is made with Burgundy, but any type of dry red wine will do. Filled with tender rabbit pieces, mushrooms, carrots, and onions, the red wine ties everything together. The bacon gives a rich taste to the stew while adding some fattiness to the otherwise lean rabbit meat.

Yield: 6 servings

2 bone-in rabbits, approximately 2–2½ pounds (900 g to 1.1 kg) each, silver skin removed, cut into 5 pieces

6 slices bacon, diced

1 tablespoon (15 ml) extra-virgin olive oil

1 tablespoon (14 g) butter

3 large carrots, peeled and cut into ½-inch (1.3 cm) pieces

2 medium onions, roughly chopped

8 ounces (225 g) fresh small white or brown mushrooms, quartered

2 tablespoons (16 g) all-purpose flour

1½ cups (355 ml) dry red wine

1½ cups (355 ml) beef broth

2 tablespoons (32 g) tomato paste

4 garlic cloves, minced

1 teaspoon finely chopped fresh thyme

2 tablespoons (8 g) chopped fresh parsley

2 bay leaves

½ teaspoon kosher salt

¼ teaspoon black pepper

1 Place the rabbit onto a cutting board. Remove any silver skin and cut into five pieces: front and hindquarters, plus saddle. Pat dry with a paper towel.

2 In a large Dutch oven or heavy-based pot, sauté the bacon over medium heat in 1 tablespoon (15 ml) of olive oil for about 3 minutes until crisp and browned. Transfer with a slotted spoon to a large dish and set aside.

3 In the same pot, sear the rabbit pieces on all sides until browned, 2–3 minutes. Remove and place on the dish with the bacon.

4 Add the butter into the pot and allow to melt. Add the carrots, onions, and mushrooms and sauté for 2–3 minutes until just starting to become tender. Sprinkle with flour and then sauté for another minute, mixing constantly.

5 Add the red wine to the pot, scraping the sides and bottom of the pot to remove any browned bits. Mix in the beef broth and tomato paste. Bring to a boil. Add the garlic, thyme, half of the parsley, bay leaves, salt, and pepper. Bring to a boil.

6 Add the rabbit and bacon back to the pot and stir and then reduce the heat to a simmer. Cover and let cook for 1 to 1½ hours or until the rabbit is tender.

7 Remove the bay leaves. Garnish with the remaining chopped fresh parsley. Serve with bread or mashed potatoes.

BRAISED FRENCH ONION PHEASANT

Who doesn't love French onion soup? It's packed with perfectly caramelized onions and covered in gooey cheese. This Braised French Onion Pheasant is my rendition of the classic soup transformed into a savory one-pot dinner. The pheasant becomes tender and juicy as it braises in the pot of caramelized onions, garlic, and thyme. It's a rich dish without being overly heavy or complicated to make. This meal is best served over a bed of mashed potatoes with a big piece of bread.

Yield: 4 servings

1½ (25 ml) tablespoons extra-virgin olive oil

4 boneless, skinless pheasant breasts, approximately 4–5 ounces (115 to 140 g) each

½ teaspoon black pepper

2 teaspoons salt, divided

2 tablespoons (28 g) butter

2 medium sweet onions, sliced into ¼-inch (6 mm) pieces

2 garlic cloves, chopped

1 teaspoon dried thyme

1 sprig fresh rosemary

⅓ cup (80 ml) white wine

1½ (355 ml) cups chicken broth

1 tablespoon (15 ml) balsamic vinegar

1 teaspoon Worcestershire sauce

1 tablespoon (15 g) Dijon mustard

1 cup (120 g) shredded Gruyère cheese

1 Preheat the oven to 375°F (190°C, or gas mark 5).

2 Heat the olive oil in a large ovenproof skillet over medium heat. Season the pheasant with pepper and 1 teaspoon salt. Sear in the olive oil until golden brown on both sides, about 2 minutes on each side. Remove from the skillet and transfer the pheasant to a plate.

3 In the same pan, add the butter and allow to melt. Add the onions and reduce the heat to low. Cook the onions low and slow for about 15 minutes, stirring occasionally, until golden and caramelized.

4 Once the onions are caramel in color, add the garlic, thyme, rosemary, and remaining salt. Cook for 3 minutes.

5 Remove the rosemary sprig. Increase the heat to high and add the wine. Bring to a boil and cook until reduced by half, about 3–5 minutes.

6 Add the chicken broth, balsamic vinegar, Worcestershire sauce, and Dijon mustard and then reduce to a simmer and cook for an additional 10 minutes.

7 Add the pheasant back into the pan. Bake uncovered on the center rack of the preheated oven for 15 minutes.

8 Sprinkle the pheasant with Gruyère cheese and place back into the oven under the broiler. Watch carefully so the cheese doesn't burn.

9 Once the cheese is melted, remove from the oven and serve.

SLOW-COOKER GARLIC-SESAME VENISON AND BROCCOLI

Chances are you have enjoyed the Chinese takeout staple beef and broccoli at some point. My version of its delicious sauce combines garlic, soy sauce, sesame oil, brown sugar, rice vinegar, and a pinch of crushed red pepper. This dish also has a slightly different signature flavor because it trades beef for tender and juicy venison chunks. Venison is a great swap because it's a much leaner meat than beef. While just about any cut can work well, this recipe is a great one for using up less prime cuts, such as the ones from the deer's front quarters. This dish is sure to be a weeknight hit for the entire family.

Yield: 4 servings

3 pound (1.4 kg) venison roast, cut into bite-sized pieces

1 white onion, julienned

3 green onions, white and green parts, sliced, plus more for serving

¼ cup (60 ml) cold water

1 tablespoon (8 g) cornstarch

1 bag (10 ounces, or 280 g) microwavable broccoli florets

Sesame seeds, for garnish

MARINADE

4 tablespoons (40 g) minced garlic

½ cup (120 ml) low-sodium soy sauce

¼ cup (60 ml) sesame oil

2 tablespoons (30 g) brown sugar

1 tablespoon (15 ml) rice vinegar

½ teaspoon crushed red pepper

1 Combine the marinade ingredients in a large bowl and add the venison pieces. Marinate overnight or for at least 1 hour in the refrigerator.

2 Pour the venison and marinade into a greased slow cooker along with the white onion and green onions. Cover and cook on low for 4–5 hours.

3 About 30 minutes before serving, whisk together the cold water and cornstarch. Add the cornstarch slurry to the slow cooker and stir. Cover and cook on high for another 30 minutes or so.

4 Prepare the broccoli according to the microwave directions. Stir in the cooked broccoli and mix until the sauce is evenly distributed.

5 Serve over cooked white rice and sprinkle with sesame seeds and more sliced green onions.

SLOW COOKER VENISON BARBACOA

Barbacoa is a savory Mexican-style dish with flavors of chili powder, oregano, and cumin. There is a punch of acidity, which I get in this recipe from the apple cider vinegar and lime juice. While barbacoa is most often beef or lamb, the cooking technique is great for venison as it turns out extra tender when cooked low and slow. Venison barbacoa is a very versatile dish that's great at any time of the year, but I especially love to serve this dish during the summer months as the star in a taco spread.

Yield: 4–6 servings

1 large yellow onion

2–4 chipotle peppers in adobo sauce

2 tablespoons (36 g) salt

5-pound (2.3 kg) venison neck roast, or another large roast

3 garlic cloves, minced

1 tablespoon (8 g) chili powder

1 tablespoon (3 g) dried oregano

1 teaspoon ground cumin

¼ cup (60 ml) green hot sauce

½ cup (120 ml) freshly squeezed lime juice

2 tablespoons (28 ml) apple cider vinegar

1½ cups (355 ml) beef broth

Chopped fresh cilantro, for garnish

1   Cut the onion and the chipotle peppers into long, thin strips.

2   Salt all sides of the roast liberally and then place the venison roast, onion, chipotle peppers, and garlic into a slow cooker. Add the seasonings directly to the meat.

3   Add the green hot sauce, lime juice, apple cider vinegar, and beef broth.

4   Cook for 4–6 hours on low.

5   The meat is done when it starts to fall apart. Shred with two forks.

6   Garnish with chopped fresh cilantro and serve over white rice, in tacos, or in a bun.

VENISON VS. BEEF

A lot of people compare venison with beef. In many ways, the two are very similar, but there are distinct differences as well. Deer are much leaner than beef cattle; therefore, venison has a lower fat content and fewer calories. The fat in beef carries a flavor many people enjoy, but for venison, it's the exact opposite. The fat is what gives venison a "gamey" flavor, and it is best to trim off any fat. Venison also does not carry marbling like we see in beef. Because of this, venison loses its moisture faster. So, cooking venison improperly can make it dry out quickly. One way to trap in moisture is by cooking it low and slow. Cooking a roast in a slow cooker surrounded by liquid helps trap the moisture, leaving you with a juicy and tender wild game dinner.

SLOW COOKER WILD TURKEY AND STUFFING

With this dish, you get all of the delicious flavors of Thanksgiving Day with only a portion of the work. And while it cooks for hours, this dish takes only minutes to prepare. The tender wild turkey breast, stuffing, cream of chicken soup, sour cream, vegetables, and chicken broth come together to create an irresistible meal that reminds you of the holidays.

Yield: 4 servings

1 wild boneless, skinless turkey breast, approximately 2 pounds (900 g)

1 teaspoon salt

2 teaspoons dry rosemary

1 box (6 ounces, or 170 g) stuffing mix

1 can (10½ ounces, or 300 g) condensed cream of chicken soup

8 ounces (225 g) sour cream

½ cup (120 ml) low-sodium chicken broth, divided

1 bag (10 ounces, or 280 g) frozen green beans

½ cup (80 g) onions, diced

½ cup (50 g) celery, diced

Turkey gravy, powdered mix or jarred, for serving

1 Cut the wild turkey breast into three or four equal pieces, similar in size to a standard chicken breast. Season the pieces with salt and rosemary. Place on the bottom of a lightly greased slow cooker.

2 In a large bowl, combine the stuffing mix, condensed soup, sour cream, and chicken broth. Transfer into the slow cooker.

3 Add the green beans, onion, and celery and cook on low for 6–7 hours or on high for 4 hours.

4 When the turkey is almost done, prepare or heat the turkey gravy.

5 Remove the turkey and shred using two forks. Mix back into the stuffing mixture.

6 Serve topped with the hot turkey gravy.

SMOKED CANADA GOOSE PASTRAMI

There are many people who for whatever reason don't like the taste of wild goose. If you're one of the haters, I think this recipe will change your mind. Homemade pastrami like this can make a statement on charcuterie boards. It also tastes great on Reuben sandwiches or even as a snack, eaten on its own. There is a lot of size variation with Canada geese. It is important to weigh your goose breasts and adjust the salt accordingly.

Yield: 3–4 servings

GOOSE

2 skinless, boneless goose breasts, approximately 1½ pounds (680 g)

DRY BRINE

1 tablespoon curing salt per 1 pound (455 g) of meat (I use Morton's Tender Quick.)

¼ cup (60 g) brown sugar

3 tablespoons (18 g) black pepper

1 tablespoon (11 g) whole mustard seed

2 tablespoons (20 g) granulated garlic

2 teaspoons onion powder

2 teaspoons dried thyme

RUB

2 tablespoons (12 g) cracked black pepper

2 tablespoons (30 g) brown sugar

1 teaspoon ground coriander

½ teaspoon granulated garlic

½ teaspoon onion powder

½ teaspoon paprika

¼ teaspoon crushed red pepper (optional)

1   Weigh the goose breasts and adjust the amount of tenderizing salt. Rinse the breasts and pat dry with a paper towel.

2   Combine all the ingredients for the dry brine in a small bowl and mix using your hands. Rub the marinade into the goose breasts. Place into a resealable plastic bag and remove any air. Place into the refrigerator and brine for 72 hours, flipping every day.

3   After the brining time is finished, rinse the breasts thoroughly. Place the breasts into a bowl of cold water in the refrigerator for 30 minutes to draw some of the salt out. Rinse well with water after taking the breasts out of the cold water bath.

4   While the goose is resting in the refrigerator, preheat your smoker to 225°F (107°C).

5   In a medium-sized bowl, combine the rub ingredients. Pat the goose breasts dry with a paper towel and then season with the rub. If you prefer a less spicy option, either cut the crushed red pepper or omit it completely.

6   Once the smoker is preheated, place the goose breasts into the smoker and cook until the internal temperature reaches 150°F (65.5°C). This process takes approximately 1 hour but varies depending on the size of your Canada goose breasts.

7   Remove the goose pastrami from the smoker and it rest for 30 minutes.

8   Slice thin and serve.

LEMON CAPER BRAISED RABBIT

Rabbit is considered a dryer game meat that can often be challenging to cook. But I've found braising rabbit is the foolproof way to prepare it! In this recipe, the rabbit pieces are seared and then braised in a mixture of white wine and broth. The Sauvignon Blanc adds zip to the lemon-and-caper-infused liquid. Once fully cooked, the rabbit pieces should be so tender that they fall apart with the touch of fork. This dish is best served with good bread so you can soak up that delicious braising liquid.

Yield: 4 servings

2 bone-in rabbits, approximately 2–2½ pounds (900 g to 1.1 kg) each, silver skin removed, each rabbit cut into 5 pieces

1 teaspoon kosher salt

2 tablespoons (16 g) all-purpose flour, for dusting

4 tablespoons (60 ml) extra-virgin olive oil, divided

1 large onion, finely diced

1 garlic clove, finely diced

½ cup (120 ml) dry white wine (such as Sauvignon Blanc)

1 cup (235 ml) low-sodium chicken broth

1 lemon

1 bay leaf

½ cup (30 g) minced fresh flat-leaf parsley, plus more for garnish

2 sprigs fresh thyme

2 tablespoons (18 g) capers, drained

¼ teaspoon black pepper

1 Preheat the oven to 350°F (180°C, or gas mark 4).

2 Pat the rabbit dry with paper towels and season with salt on both sides. Dust with flour.

3 Heat 2 tablespoons (28 ml) of olive oil in an ovenproof skillet over medium-high heat. Once the oil is shimmering, place the rabbit into the pan and brown on both sides, approximately 4 minutes per side. Remove from the pan and set aside.

4 Add the remaining olive oil to the same skillet. Add the onion and cook until translucent, 3–4 minutes. Stir often.

5 Add the garlic and cook until fragrant, approximately 1 minute.

6 Add the wine and bring to a boil over high heat. Heat until reduced by half, approximately 5 minutes. Add the chicken broth, juice from half of the lemon, the bay leaf, parsley, thyme, and capers. Bring to a boil.

7 While your skillet starts to boil, slice the remaining lemon half into slices, about ¼ inch (6 mm).

8 Once boiling, remove the bay leaf and thyme sprigs. Add the rabbit back into the skillet and scatter the lemon slices around. Place into the oven and cook for 30 minutes or until the rabbit is tender.

9 Remove the bay leaf and season with ¼ teaspoon pepper.

10 Garnish with minced fresh parsley and serve.

4

BAKED AND FRIED

Venison Lasagna... 103

Venison Chili Mac and Cheese 105

White Enchiladas with Wild Turkey 109

Barbecue Venison Crescent Ring Pizza 111

Philly Cheesesteak Stuffed Shells.................................. 113

Baked Venison Meatballs with Penne
All'Arrabbiata Sauce 115

Wild Game Tater Tot Casserole.. 117

Wild Turkey Cordon Bleu... 119

Buffalo-Garlic-Barbecue Fried Turkey Tenders 121

Chicken-Fried Venison... 123

Fried Pheasant Sandwich 125

Pan-Fried Duck Dumplings.. 127

Cajun Gator Nuggets.. 129

Pan-Fried Deer Heart with Peppers and Onions 131

VENISON LASAGNA

Lasagna is an easy way to feed a crowd, and it's equally tasty with venison. One pound (455 g) of meat seems standard in most lasagna recipes, but being a meat lover, I thought a little extra was in order. Lasagna is great because it brings together all of the things we love in a good pasta dish: noodles, cheeses, fresh herbs, and a delicious meat sauce. As in a couple other recipes, I blend in some pork so that there's enough fat (venison on its own is too lean to be "rich" enough in this dish).

Yield: 12 servings

LASAGNA

12 lasagna noodles

8 ounces (225 g) shredded mozzarella cheese

¼ cup (25 g) grated Parmesan cheese

2 tablespoons fresh (6 g) basil or (8 g) parsley, for garnish

MEAT SAUCE

1 pound (455 g) ground venison

½ pound (225 g) ground pork (or wild hog)

1 medium onion, diced

4 garlic cloves, minced

1 tablespoon (6 g) Italian seasoning

1 teaspoon dried oregano

1 teaspoon garlic powder

1 teaspoon onion powder

½ teaspoon paprika

½ teaspoon salt

½ teaspoon black pepper

1 tablespoon (13 g) sugar

1 jar (32 ounces, or 910 g) pasta sauce

CHEESE FILLING

2 cups (500 g) ricotta cheese

1 cup (115 g) shredded mozzarella cheese

½ cup (50 g) grated Parmesan cheese

¼ cup (15 g) chopped fresh parsley

2 tablespoons (6 g) chopped fresh basil

1 In a large pan over medium-high heat, brown the ground venison, ground pork, and onion until no pink remains, approximately 10 minutes. Stir often.

2 Add the garlic and cook until fragrant, approximately 1 minute.

3 Add the seasonings, sugar, and half of the jarred pasta sauce (approximately 1¾ cups [410 ml]). Reduce the heat to low while preparing the lasagna noodles and cheese filling.

4 To prepare the cheese filling, combine the ricotta cheese, 1 cup (115 g) of mozzarella cheese, Parmesan cheese, parsley, and basil in a medium-sized bowl. Stir until evenly mixed.

5 Preheat the oven to 375°F (190°C, or gas mark 5).

6 Cook the pasta al dente according to package directions. Rinse under cold water and set aside.

7 Get out a 9- x 13-inch (23 x 33 cm) baking dish. You should have half of the jarred pasta sauce left. Use half of what's remaining (approximately ¾ cup [170 ml]) to cover the bottom of the dish. You will use the rest for the top layer.

8 Layer four lasagna noodles on top of the pasta sauce. Top with the meat sauce, then lasagna noodles, and then cheese mixture. Repeat until you use up all the ingredients.

9 For the final layer, pour the rest of the jarred pasta sauce (approximately ¾ cup [170 ml]) over the top of the lasagna noodles. Use the back end of a spoon to distribute the sauce evenly over the lasagna noodles. Top with 8 ounces (225 g) of mozzarella cheese and bake for 40 minutes, covered with greased tinfoil. Remove the tinfoil and bake for another 10 minutes.

10 Sprinkle Parmesan cheese over top, garnish with fresh chopped parsley or basil, and serve.

VENISON CHILI MAC AND CHEESE

Talk about a meal mash-up! This chili mac and cheese recipe has a thick and flavorful homemade chili combined with classic, creamy mac and cheese. It has that delicious chili spice mix you get when you combine cumin, chili powder, and paprika. While the chili simmers, you cook the mac and cheese and then fuse them together to create a zesty, hearty dish. It might seem unusual if chili mac doesn't have a history in your part of the country, but once you try this recipe, you'll be a believer—and probably start dreaming up all sorts of variations.

Yield: 6–8 servings

CHILI

1 tablespoon (15 ml) extra-virgin olive oil

1 pound (455 g) ground venison

1 large yellow onion, diced

1 green pepper, seeded and diced

3 garlic cloves, minced

1 tablespoon (8 g) chili powder

½ teaspoon smoked paprika

1 teaspoon dried cumin

1 tablespoon (16 g) tomato paste

8 ounces (225 g) tomato sauce

1 can (10 ounces, or 280 g) tomato and diced chilies

½ cup (120 ml) beef broth

1 can (15½ ounces, or 440 g) red kidney beans, drained

MAKE THE CHILI

1 In a large pot over medium heat, heat the olive oil and then cook and crumble the ground venison for 2 minutes. Add the onion and cook for 5 more minutes or until the venison is brown and the onions are soft. Drain any grease. Add the green peppers and garlic and cook until the green peppers are softened, about 4 minutes.

2 Add the seasonings and tomato paste and stir to combine. Allow to cook for 1 minute. Add the tomato sauce, diced tomatoes and green chiles, and beef broth. Stir to combine.

3 Bring to a boil and then reduce to a light simmer. Partially cover while you prepare the macaroni and cheese. The longer it simmers, the thicker and more concentrated it will get. Add the drained kidney beans during the last 10 minutes or so.

(Continued on next page)

(Continued from previous page)

. . . .

MAC AND CHEESE

2 tablespoons (28 g) butter

2 tablespoons (16 g) all-purpose flour

½ cup (120 ml) heavy cream

1 cup (235 ml) whole milk

8 ounces (225 g) processed cheese, cubed (I use Velveeta.)

1 cup (115 g) shredded Monterey Jack cheese

1 teaspoon salt

1 package (16 ounces, or 455 g) elbow macaroni pasta, cooked to al dente and drained

TOPPING

½ cup (58 g) shredded cheddar cheese

½ cup (58 g) shredded Monterey Jack cheese

Chopped fresh parsley, for garnish

MAKE THE MACARONI AND CHEESE

1 Preheat the oven to 400°F (200°C, or gas mark 6).

2 Melt the butter in a 4½- to 5-quart (4.3 to 4.7 L) Dutch oven or large soup pot over medium heat.

3 Once the butter has melted and is starting to bubble, whisk in the flour and stir continuously for 2 minutes.

4 Add the heavy cream in splashes, stirring continuously. Then, add the milk using the same process.

5 Bring the mixture to a boil and then reduce to a simmer. Gradually add the processed cheese and Monterey Jack cheese, stirring continuously, until well combined and smooth. Season with salt and mix in the cooked elbow macaroni.

6 Add the chili to the macaroni and gently stir to combine. Once mixed, top with a ½ cup (58 g) each of cheddar cheese and Monterey Jack cheese and bake uncovered for 15–20 minutes or until the cheese is melted.

7 Garnish with chopped fresh parsley and serve!

HUNTING WILD TURKEYS

Springtime means one thing in my house: turkey hunting! It's hard to explain to people who don't get into turkey hunting just how exciting it is to set up those first decoys.

If you've never been, it goes something like this: The weather is beginning to warm up, the fields are turning green, and the flowers are just starting to bloom. But more than the sights or the smells, it's the sounds of turkey hunting that make it so unique. As the sun comes up, you begin hearing gobbles from all directions. As a turkey makes his way to your calls, he is usually gobbling his head off. He struts his way over, with his feathers fully puffed out. To me, this is when things seem to move in slow motion. As he puts on his final show, he dances so gracefully around the decoys. It's time to prepare to take my shot. Then, it's over quick. All is silent, at least for a moment.

WHITE ENCHILADAS WITH WILD TURKEY

This recipe is a great way to use the leg and thigh meat from your turkey, but you could just as easily swap it out and use breast meat if you want. You start by cooking the meat in a slow cooker with seasonings and chicken broth to create the most tender pull-apart wild turkey. So, keep in mind that you'll need to get the turkey going 4–8 hours before you want to cook this recipe. Once shredded, the turkey gets mixed with cheese and green onions and is used to fill the enchiladas that then get covered in a mouthwatering green chile sauce and topped with yet more Monterey Jack cheese. It's an irresistible combination.

Yield: 8 servings

2 wild turkey leg and thigh portions, or 1 boneless, skinless wild turkey breast, approximately 2 pounds (900 g)

2 teaspoons garlic powder

1 teaspoon salt

½ teaspoon black pepper

2 teaspoons dried oregano

4 cups (950 ml) chicken broth

ENCHILADAS

2½ cups (288 g) shredded Monterey Jack cheese, divided

2–3 tablespoons (12 to 18 g) green onions, sliced, white parts and green parts separated

8–10 flour tortillas (8 inches, or 20 cm)

3 tablespoons (42 g) butter

3 tablespoons (24 g) all-purpose flour

2 cups (475 ml) chicken broth

1 cup (230 g) sour cream

2 cans (4 ounces, or 115 g each) diced green chilies

5 ounces (140 g) cream cheese, softened

½ teaspoon salt

¼ teaspoon ground cumin

1 Place the wild turkey into a slow cooker. Season with garlic powder, salt, pepper, and oregano. Pour the chicken broth over top. Cook on low for 8 hours or high for 4 hours. Remove the wild turkey from the slow cooker and shred with two forks. Discard any bones if using leg and thighs.

2 Preheat the oven to 350°F (180°C, or gas mark 4).

3 In a large bowl, combine the shredded turkey, 1 cup (115 g) of Monterey Jack cheese, and the white parts of the green onions.

4 Assemble the enchiladas by filling each tortilla evenly with the shredded turkey mixture. Roll the tortillas tightly to close and place seam-side down in a 9- x 13-inch (23 x 33 cm) baking dish.

5 In a medium saucepan, melt the butter over medium heat. Add the flour and whisk together until smooth. Cook, whisking constantly, for 1 minute.

6 Slowly whisk in the 2 cups (475 ml) of chicken broth and bring to a low simmer. Stir constantly.

7 Add the sour cream, green chiles, cream cheese, 1 cup (115 g) of Monterey Jack cheese, ½ teaspoon salt, and ground cumin. Stir together until the cheese has completely melted and the sauce is bubbling. Remove from the heat.

8 Pour the sauce over the enchiladas and top with the remaining ½ cup (58 g) of Monterey Jack cheese.

9 Bake for 30 minutes or until done. The cheese should be bubbly and the corners of the tortillas should be a nice golden brown color.

10 Garnish with green parts of the green onions and serve immediately.

BARBECUE VENISON CRESCENT RING PIZZA

Cheesy and filled with wild game meat, this crescent ring is very much like a stromboli, only flaky thanks to the crescent dough. It is perfect for the family or a game night with friends. Pastry can be complicated, but we're using store-bought dough to keep it as simple as it gets. Ground venison is smothered in your favorite barbecue sauce, spooned into a ring of crescent rolls, and layered with mozzarella cheese and red onion. It then gets baked in the oven until its edges are slightly crisp and golden brown. Slice, dip, and eat!

Yield: 4–6 servings

1 tablespoon (15 ml) extra-virgin olive oil

1 pound (455 g) ground venison

1 cup (250 g) barbecue sauce

2 tubes (8 ounces, or 225 g each) refrigerated crescent roll dough

½ cup (80 g) thinly sliced red onion

1 cup (115 g) shredded mozzarella cheese

Ranch dressing, for dipping

1 Preheat the oven to 375°F (190°C, or gas mark 5).

2 Heat the olive oil in a nonstick skillet. Add the ground venison and cook until just browned, breaking it up with a spatula as it cooks, 5–7 minutes. Add the barbecue sauce and simmer for 5 minutes. Remove from the heat.

3 Coat a baking sheet with nonstick cooking spray. Lay out both packs of the crescent rolls with the pointed ends facing the edge of the baking sheet. Use a small bowl to create a circle in the middle. The rolls will overlap near the center.

4 Spoon the barbecue venison onto the rolls toward the center of the ring. Sprinkle red onion on top and then sprinkle mozzarella cheese over top.

5 Pull the pointed part of the rolls over the filling and tuck the ends under the center part of the roll. (You will be able to see some of the filling but that is okay.)

6 Bake in the oven for about 20 minutes or until the crescent rolls are a golden brown.

7 Serve with ranch dressing for dipping.

PHILLY CHEESESTEAK STUFFED SHELLS

One of the recipes that went viral almost immediately was my Venison Philly Cheesesteak Stuffed Peppers. While I still make that recipe, I have also played with variations and now, I have to admit, this recipe just might have that one beat. It's pasta filled with game meat, bell peppers, and onions and smothered in cheese sauce . . . what could possibly go wrong?

Yield: 6 servings

24 jumbo pasta shells

1 tablespoon (14 g) butter

1 pound (455 g) ground venison

1 small yellow onion, diced

2 green bell pepper, seeded and diced

½ teaspoon salt

½ teaspoon black pepper

1 teaspoon garlic powder

1 teaspoon onion powder

2 tablespoons (30 g) ketchup

2 tablespoons (28 ml) Worcestershire sauce

1 cup (235 ml) beef broth

1 cup (235 ml) whole milk

1 tablespoon (8 g) cornstarch

4 ounces (115 g) cream cheese

8 ounces (225 g) shredded cheddar cheese

1 Boil water in a large pot. Cook the pasta shells al dente according to package directions.

2 Preheat the oven to 350°F (180°C, or gas mark 4).

3 In a large skillet, melt 1 tablespoon (14 g) of butter over medium heat. Add the ground venison, onion, and bell peppers. Cook until the venison is browned, about 5 minutes. As it cooks, use a spatula to break up the meat into crumbles and stir often.

4 Add the salt, pepper, garlic powder, and onion powder. Mix well and then add the ketchup and Worcestershire sauce. Cook for an additional 2 minutes and then turn off the heat.

5 Fill the cooked pasta shells with the meat mixture and place in an even layer in a baking dish.

6 Using the same pan, add the beef broth, milk, and cornstarch and whisk and bring to a light simmer.

7 Add the cream cheese and cheddar cheese a little at a time, while whisking, and cook for 3–5 minutes or until thickened.

8 Pour the sauce over the shells and place the baking dish in the oven and cook for 15 minutes or until the cheese melts.

9 Once melted, remove from the oven and serve immediately.

BAKED VENISON MEATBALLS WITH PENNE ALL'ARRABBIATA SAUCE

This Italian dinner is a spicy homemade red pasta sauce paired with penne pasta and big wild game meatballs. To make the meatballs, you combine lean venison with rich hot Italian sausage. The blend of meats helps give the venison more flavor and also adds fat. But it's the egg and the bread crumbs that keep the meatballs from becoming too dry or falling apart. While you can make the sauce ahead of time, it's actually quick enough to throw together while the meatballs bake! But don't let the short cook time fool you; it's not lacking in flavor. As the tomatoes simmer and reduce, the meatballs should be about finished in the oven. Once the timing lines up, just add the meatballs to the sauce and let it continue to simmer for just 10 minutes. Then, dinner is served!

Yield: 4–6 servings

MEATBALLS

1½ pounds (680 g) ground venison

½ pound (225 g) ground hot Italian sausage

½ cup (80 g) finely chopped onion

4 garlic cloves, minced

2 large eggs, lightly beaten

⅔ cup (75 g) Italian-style panko bread crumbs

¼ cup (25 g) grated Parmesan cheese

½ teaspoon salt

1 teaspoon paprika

2 tablespoons (12 g) Italian seasoning

ARRABBIATA SAUCE

4 tablespoons (55 g) unsalted butter

½ yellow onion, finely diced

5 garlic cloves, minced

2 tablespoons (32 g) tomato paste

¼ teaspoon crushed red pepper, more or less depending on desired spiciness

½ teaspoon salt

½ teaspoon black pepper

¼ cup (10 g) chopped fresh basil

1 teaspoon dried oregano

3 cans (28 ounces, or 785 g each) San Marzano tomatoes (with juice)

PENNE

1 pound (455 g) penne rigate, cooked to al dente

½ cup (50 g) grated Parmesan cheese

Chopped fresh basil, for garnish

MAKE THE MEATBALLS

1 Preheat the oven to 400°F (200°C, or gas mark 6).

2 Mix all the ingredients for the meatballs in a bowl thoroughly. Roll into 16 balls and arrange on a baking sheet or pan with sides. Bake for 20 minutes. Turn at least once.

MAKE THE ARRABBIATA SAUCE

1 In a large pot, heat the butter over medium-high and add the onion and garlic and sauté for 3 minutes.

2 Reduce the heat to medium and add the tomato paste and seasonings and sauté for 2 minutes.

3 Add the tomatoes, stir, and simmer until reduced slightly, about 10 minutes.

4 Add the cooked meatballs and simmer for another 10 minutes. Season the sauce with more salt to taste. Add the cooked penne.

5 Garnish with Parmesan cheese and chopped fresh basil and serve.

WILD GAME TATER TOT CASSEROLE

Here's my take on America's "cowboy casserole." I've found with tater tots as a base, you're sure to make an easy weeknight dish the whole family will like enough to get second helpings. My recipe is layered with ground game meat, of course, along with creamy mushroom sauce, spinach, corn, and cheese. Oh, and for the finishing touches, I recommend a sprinkle of Parmesan cheese, bacon pieces, and chopped greens, but you can also make a "toppings bar" and let each person choose their own.

Yield: 8 servings

1 bag (32 ounces, or 905 g) tater tots

1 tablespoon (14 g) butter or (15 ml) vegetable or peanut oil

1 medium yellow onion, diced

2 garlic cloves, chopped

1 pound (455 g) ground venison

1 can (10.75 ounces, or 305 g) condensed cream of mushroom soup

⅓ cup (80 ml) whole milk

¼ cup (60 g) sour cream

½ teaspoon salt

½ teaspoon black pepper, divided

2 cups (60 g) baby spinach, roughly chopped

1 cup (164 g) frozen corn

1 bag (8 ounces, or 225 g) shredded cheddar cheese

¼ cup (25 g) grated Parmesan cheese

Nonstick cooking spray

4 strips bacon

Chopped chives or scallions, for garnish

1 Preheat the oven to 375°F (190°C, or gas mark 5).

2 Remove the tater tots from the freezer to let them thaw slightly while you prepare the filling.

3 Heat 1 tablespoon (14 g) of butter or (15 ml) oil in a large skillet over medium heat. Add the onion to the skillet and cook until slightly softened, about 4 minutes. Add the garlic and cook for 1 more minute. Add the ground venison and break into small pieces with a wooden spoon. Cook the meat until no pink remains, 6–8 minutes.

4 Stir in the mushroom soup, milk, sour cream, salt, and pepper and mix until smooth. Fold in the spinach to wilt slightly and then add the corn.

5 Sprinkle the cheddar cheese evenly over the top of the casserole. Place the tater tots on top in a single layer. Spray with nonstick cooking spray and then sprinkle the top with Parmesan cheese.

6 Bake in the oven for 30–35 minutes or until the tater tots are fully cooked and crispy.

7 While the casserole is baking, cook the bacon until crispy. Once the casserole is done, remove from the oven and crumble the cooked bacon over top. Let rest 5 minutes.

8 Garnish with chopped chives or scallions and serve.

WILD TURKEY CORDON BLEU

Cordon bleu is a classic recipe in which breaded meat is wrapped around a cheese stuffing and either fried or baked. The traditional version incorporates a thin layer of Serrano ham between the layers of meat and cheese. My mom used to make this dish all the time, and I loved it! For my own Wild Turkey Cordon Bleu recipe, I used wild turkey breast and a thinly sliced prosciutto. For the cheese, I chose Brie and Swiss. And instead of sticking with a more traditional dish, I decided to add a rich Dijon cream sauce as well! I think you'll love it with the wild turkey.

Yield: 5–7 servings

1 boneless, skinless wild turkey breast, approximately 2 pounds (900 g)

½ teaspoon salt

¼ teaspoon black pepper

1 teaspoon smoked paprika

1 teaspoon garlic powder

6 slices prosciutto

4 slices Swiss cheese

8 ounces (225 g) Brie, cut into slices

½ cup (63 g) all-purpose flour

1–2 large eggs, beaten

1 cup (112 g) Italian-style panko bread crumbs

¼ cup (25 g) grated Parmesan cheese

Nonstick cooking spray

SAUCE

2 tablespoons of (28 g) butter

1½ tablespoons (12 g) all-purpose flour

2 cups (475 ml) whole milk

2 tablespoons (30 g) Dijon mustard

1 teaspoon garlic powder

⅓ cup (33 g) grated Parmesan cheese

1. Preheat the oven to 350°F (180°C, or gas mark 4).

2. Butterfly the breast and then cover the wild turkey breast with plastic wrap and pound the meat into an even thickness, approximately ¼-inch (6 mm) thick.

3. Season the wild turkey breast with salt, pepper, paprika, and garlic powder. Layer the prosciutto evenly over the breast meat. Place the Swiss cheese and Brie down the center of the meat and roll tightly around the cheese. Pin the roll together with toothpicks.

4. Prepare three shallow dishes for coating. The first dish will contain the flour. The second dish will have the egg wash. For the final dish, mix the panko and Parmesan cheese. Roll the turkey breast into each one of these shallow dishes in that order.

5. Place onto a baking dish, spray with nonstick cooking spray, and cook in the oven until the coating is golden brown and crunchy and the interior reads 165°F (74°C) on an instant read or remote thermometer. On average, this should take 45 minutes. Larger turkey breasts may take an hour to be fully cooked.

6. While the cordon bleu is baking, start preparing the sauce. In a medium saucepan, melt the butter over medium-high heat. Add the flour and constantly whisk until it turns into a thick golden roux. Slowly add the milk, keeping the sauce at a simmer. Stir in the Dijon mustard, garlic powder, and Parmesan cheese. Reduce the heat to low while the cordon bleu finishes baking. Stir often.

7. Let the cordon bleu rest for 10 minutes before removing the toothpicks.

8. Slice and serve with the warm sauce.

BUFFALO-GARLIC-BARBECUE FRIED TURKEY TENDERS

This sauce is my absolute all-time favorite! There is something about mixing hot sauce and barbecue sauce that creates an amazing flavor combination. For this recipe, I rely on store-bought buffalo sauce but make my own barbecue sauce. For the wild turkey tenders, I tested them a few different ways, but I ended up liking them best when coated in seasoned flour, then dredged in an egg wash, and then coated with another round of seasoned flour. After they are fried to the perfect golden tender, try a bite on its own and then dip, dunk, or smother away.

Yield: 2 turkey tenders per serving

6 to 8 wild turkey breast tenders

4 cups (576 g) seasoned flour (such as Kentucky Kernel), divided

2 large eggs, beaten with ¼ cup (60 ml) water

Vegetable or peanut oil, for frying

BUFFALO-GARLIC-BARBECUE SAUCE

1 tablespoon (14 g) butter

½ cup (120 ml) buffalo sauce (I prefer Frank's Red Hot Buffalo Wings Sauce.)

2 tablespoons (28 ml) apple cider vinegar

1 tablespoon (15 g) brown sugar

1 teaspoon ketchup

3 garlic cloves, minced

¼ teaspoon onion powder

1   First, make the sauce. Melt the butter in a small saucepan over medium heat. Add all the ingredients for the sauce and stir well. Bring the mixture to a light boil. Reduce the heat to low and maintain the sauce at a simmer while you fry the wild turkey tenders.

2   To fry the tenders, start by assembling a breading station with three shallow bowls. The first station will have 2 cups (288 g) of flour, the second will have the egg wash, and the third will be another flour station with the remaining 2 cups (288 g) of flour.

3   Heat ½ inch (1.3 cm) of oil in a large skillet over medium-high heat. While the oil heats, dip each tender into the seasoned flour, then into the egg wash, making sure to coat the entire surface, and then into the second flour container.

4   Once the oil reaches 350°F (180°C), gently place the tenders into the hot skillet. Fry the turkey tenders in batches to avoid overcrowding the pan. Fry for 3–4 minutes per side or until the turkey is a crispy golden brown and is just cooked through. Transfer the cooked turkey to a paper towel–lined sheet pan.

5   You can serve the turkey tenders with the sauce on the side for dipping, or you can transfer the tenders into the skillet and coat them with the sauce.

CHICKEN-FRIED VENISON

....

This chicken-fried venison is tenderized, breaded, and fried golden brown before being smothered in a luxurious country gravy. Yes, this main dish checks all the boxes: it's comforting, crunchy, tender, and rich. The name of this dish refers to how the venison cutlet is battered and fried similar to how fried chicken is prepared. You start by soaking the venison in a salt bath, which helps tenderize the meat. If you don't deep-fry all that often, this recipe is a good introduction. Since the meat is nice and thin, it's sure to be cooked perfectly as soon as you have delicious golden brown fried batter on the outside.

Yield: 5 servings

VENISON

1–2 pounds (455 to 900 g) venison (tenderloin or backstrap)

3 cups (375 g) all-purpose flour

1 tablespoon (6 g) black pepper

¼ teaspoon ground sage

¼ teaspoon cayenne pepper

2 tablespoons (36 g) salt

3 cups (700 ml) vegetable or peanut oil, for frying

GRAVY

2 tablespoons (28 g) butter

¼ cup (32 g) all-purpose flour

¼ cup (60 ml) buttermilk

2 cups (475 ml) heavy cream

½ teaspoon kosher salt

1 tablespoon (6 g) black pepper

MAKE THE COUNTRY GRAVY

1 Melt the butter in a small saucepan set over medium-low heat. Sprinkle flour into the melted butter and whisk for 2 minutes while the raw flour taste cooks out.

2 Slowly dribble the buttermilk into the saucepan a little at a time, while continuing to stir. To prevent lumps, make sure the milk is fully incorporated before adding more. Do the same with the heavy cream. As the gravy thins out, more cream can be added at once. Continue until all the cream has been added.

3 Bring the gravy to a simmer to thicken and add salt and pepper. Taste and adjust the seasonings as desired.

4 Keep the gravy warm in the oven at 225°F (107°C) until it is ready to be served over the chicken-fried venison.

MAKE THE CHICKEN-FRIED VENISON

1 Cut the venison steaks into individual portions, approximately ¼ to ⅓ pound (115 to 152 g) each. Pound flat and tenderize with a meat mallet.

2 Heat ½ inch (1.3 cm) of oil in a cast-iron skillet over medium heat to 325°F (170°C).

3 Mix the flour, black pepper, sage, cayenne, and 2 tablespoons (36 g) of salt in a resealable plastic bag or a separate bowl or plate for coating. Place the venison into the bag and mix with your hands until the venison is evenly coated or dredge each piece of venison in the bowl with the flour mixture.

4 Place the coated venison into the preheated oil. Flip the venison after a few minutes when the underside is golden brown, 3–4 minutes.

5 Cook on the other side until cooked through. The inside of fully cooked venison will be grayish brown with no sign of red.

6 Remove the venison onto a paper towel–lined plate to drain.

7 Serve with the warm country gravy.

FRIED PHEASANT SANDWICH

It doesn't get much better than crispy and juicy fried pheasant breast on a toasted bun. But feel free to experiment with what you've got as this recipe works great with other upland birds as well! This sandwich carries a zippy tang while ensuring moist, tender meat. After frying to the perfect golden brown, it gets served up on a toasted bun with melty cheese, pickles, tomato, red onions, and lettuce.

Yield: 4 sandwiches

BRINE

¾ cup (175 ml) buttermilk

½ cup (120 ml) pickle juice

4 boneless, skinless pheasant breasts, approximately 4–5 ounces (115 to 140 g) each

BREADING AND FRYING

½ cup (63 g) all-purpose flour

1 teaspoon black pepper

1 teaspoon cayenne pepper

1 teaspoon garlic salt

Peanut oil, for frying

SANDWICH

4 slices cheddar cheese

4 brioche buns, toasted

4 slices iceberg lettuce

1 tomato, sliced

1 small red onion, thinly sliced

Pickle chips

BRINE AND BREAD THE PHEASANT

1 Combine the buttermilk and pickle juice for the brine in a large bowl. Add the pheasant breasts and submerge into the mixture. Cover and refrigerate for at least 1 hour.

2 Remove the pheasant from the refrigerator and let it sit out for 20 minutes prior to breading.

3 Combine the flour, black pepper, cayenne, and garlic salt in a shallow dish. Coat the pheasant in the breading mixture, gently shaking off any excess.

FRY THE PHEASANT

1 Heat a deep cast-iron skillet with 2 inches (5 cm) of the peanut oil to 350°F (180°C). Add the flour-coated pheasant breasts and fry for roughly 5 minutes, flipping halfway through. Check that the internal temperature has reached 165°F (74°C). Top each pheasant breast with a slice of cheddar cheese and cook for 30 seconds before removing them to a paper towel–lined plate.

MAKE THE SANDWICH

1 Serve the fried pheasant on a toasted bun with your desired toppings such as lettuce, sliced tomato, sliced red onion, and pickle chips.

SUBSTITUTING PHEASANT IN CHICKEN RECIPES

While people say a lot of different meats taste like chicken, I do think it's safe to say pheasant is very similar to chicken. That said, it's the farm-raised pheasants, "stocked birds," that have a taste that is closer to chicken than wild pheasants. A wild bird is leaner and has less fat, making its texture a bit different than chicken as well—it has a stronger grain to it. Though there are these small differences, it is easy to adapt your favorite chicken recipes to include pheasant instead. An average pheasant breast is smaller than a chicken breast though, so it is important to factor that into your cooking when making this substitute.

PAN-FRIED DUCK DUMPLINGS

These are delicious dumplings, filled with a blend of wild duck, crunchy water chestnuts, onions, baby bok choy, garlic, and fresh ginger. While these dumplings are pan-fried and then steamed, you only need one pan! I've found the secret to the most delicious dumplings is a simple swap: just swap out the water with chicken broth when you steam them!

Yield: 6 servings

2 large boneless, skinless duck breast fillets, approximately 3½–4 ounces (100 to 115 g) each, chopped, or 4 smaller duck breasts

5 water chestnuts, diced

1 baby bok choy, diced

2 green onions, chopped

1 garlic clove, minced

1 tablespoon (6 g) minced fresh ginger

1 teaspoon sesame oil

2 tablespoons (28 ml) low-sodium soy sauce

1 teaspoon rice vinegar

24 wonton wrappers

3–4 tablespoons (45 to 60 ml) vegetable or peanut oil, for frying

¼ cup (60 ml) chicken stock

DIPPING SAUCE

3 tablespoons (45 ml) rice vinegar

3 teaspoons (15 ml) low-sodium soy sauce

2 teaspoons toasted sesame oil

1 teaspoon packed light brown sugar

1 tablespoon (6 g) finely chopped green onions, for garnish

1 To a food processor, add the chopped duck meat, water chestnuts, diced bok choy, green onions, garlic, ginger, sesame oil, soy sauce, and rice vinegar to a food processor. Process until a fine stuffing is formed and then pour into a bowl, cover, and refrigerate for 30 minutes.

2 To make the dipping sauce, whisk together the rice vinegar, soy sauce, sesame oil, and brown sugar in a small bowl. Cover and refrigerate until ready to serve.

3 Moisten the edges of the wonton wrapper lightly with cold water. Fill each wrapper with a scant tablespoon (15 ml) of filling. Close each one into a half-moon, making sure there are no air pockets. Pleat the edges with your hands.

4 Heat a skillet over medium heat and add a few tablespoons (45 to 60 ml) of oil to the skillet. Place about 8–10 pot stickers into the hot pan, flat-side down, and cook for 2 minutes.

5 Flip, then slowly add a small amount of chicken stock to the pan, turn the heat down to low, cover, and steam for another 2 minutes. Remove and set onto a heatproof platter and place in a warm oven as you repeat with the remaining pot stickers.

6 Garnish with chopped green onion and serve with the dipping sauce.

CAJUN GATOR NUGGETS

No, I don't hunt gator. But I am thankful to have friends that share wild game with me when I'm in the mood to cook something I typically don't hunt myself. I've heard plenty of people talk about Cajun gator tail, so I had to create my own recipe. Yes, this recipe is simple, but sometimes those are the best ones to really highlight an unusual meat. These nuggets get fried to a beautiful golden crispy brown color and go perfect with a variety of dipping sauces. Just make sure to try one on its own first so you can let people know if alligator really "tastes like chicken" when they inevitably ask!

Yield: 6 servings

2 large eggs, beaten

1 cup (235 ml) buttermilk

2 teaspoons water

2½ cups (313 g) all-purpose flour

1½ teaspoons Cajun seasoning

1 teaspoon salt

½ teaspoon black pepper

½ teaspoon garlic powder

½ teaspoon onion powder

½ teaspoon paprika

1 pound (455 g) alligator tail meat

Vegetable or peanut oil, for frying

CAJUN AOILI

½ cup (115 g) mayonnaise (I prefer to use Duke's brand.)

1 tablespoon (15 ml) freshly squeezed lemon juice

½ teaspoon garlic powder

½ teaspoon Cajun seasoning

1 In a bowl, beat the eggs and then add the buttermilk and water.

2 In a shallow dish, add the flour and seasonings and mix to combine.

3 Cut the alligator meat into chunks. Dredge each piece in the seasoned flour, then in the egg wash, and then back into the flour mixture.

4 Heat a cast-iron skillet over medium heat and add ¼ inch (6 mm) of oil to the bottom of the pan. Once the oil has reached 350°F (180°C), add the coated chunks of alligator. Fry over medium heat until golden brown on all sides, approximately 8 minutes.

5 Remove from the oil and drain on a paper towel–lined plate.

6 Serve with the dipping sauce.

PAN-FRIED DEER HEART WITH PEPPERS AND ONIONS

Although it's often overlooked, deer heart is a delicacy. I intentionally kept this recipe simple so you can get the full delicious flavor of the heart. That said, I did make sure to add a bit of zest, with buttery garlic, onions, and bell pepper, bringing it all together.

Yield: 4 servings

1 cup (125 g) all-purpose flour

1 teaspoon onion powder

1 teaspoon garlic powder

1 deer heart, cleaned and cut into 1-inch (2.5 cm) bite-sized pieces

½ yellow onion, julienned

1 bell pepper, seeded and julienned

¼ cup (55 g) butter, divided

1 garlic clove, minced

2 tablespoons (8 g) chopped fresh parsley

½ teaspoon black pepper

¼ teaspoon salt

1   In a large bowl or resealable plastic bag, combine the flour, onion powder, and garlic powder. Add the heart pieces and toss to coat.

2   In a large skillet, cook the onion and bell pepper in 2 tablespoons (28 g) of butter until just starting to become tender, 3 minutes.

3   Melt the rest of the butter and then add the garlic and the deer heart pieces and cook for 5–7 minutes or until no pink remains. While it's cooking, season with parsley, pepper, and salt. Stir often.

4   Serve by itself or over a bed of rice.

5

GRILLED AND GRIDDLED

Reverse Seared Rib Eye of the Sky (Sandhill Crane) ... 137

Venison Steaks with Spicy Chimichurri 139

Reverse-Seared Venison Backstrap with Herb Butter... 141

Marinated Grilled Venison Tenderloin............................ 143

Venison Smash Burgers 147

Chipotle Venison Steak Kabobs 149

Apricot-Dijon Glazed Wild Turkey 151

Thai Chili Grilled Turkey Lettuce Cups............................. 153

Jamaican Jerk Pheasant 155

Honey Garlic Wild Turkey on a Stick................................. 157

Venison with Mustard Sauce.. 159

Grilled Venison Steak Diane... 161

Venison Philly Cheesesteaks 163

Simple Ramen Duck Stir-Fry.. 165

Venison Sloppy Joe Stuffed Grilled Cheese 167

Venison Birria Tacos 169

Bourbon Wild Turkey.. 171

Venison Crunchy Wraps... 173

Jalapeño Popper Quesadillas with Wild Turkey 175

Blue Cheese Venison Burgers.. 177

REVERSE SEARED RIB EYE OF THE SKY (SANDHILL CRANE)

Sandhill cranes are a species of waterfowl that make for remarkable table fare, hence their nickname "Rib Eye of the Sky." These birds can be found from Canada to Texas, and you can't miss them once you know what you're looking for: they weigh on average between 7 and 11 pounds (3.2 to 5 kg) with wingspans averaging 5 to 6 feet (1.5 to 2 m). My experience hunting them was one I'll talk about for many years. I've never seen so many birds at one time in my life. Getting to watch my dog retrieve this massive bird was just the highlight of a super-fun trip with friends.

Yield: 2–3 servings

2 boneless, skinless sandhill crane breasts, approximately 15 ounces (425 g) each

¼ cup (60 ml) extra-virgin olive oil

¼ cup (60 ml) red wine vinegar

¼ cup (60 ml) low-sodium soy sauce

¼ cup (15 g) chopped fresh parsley

1 tablespoon (15 ml) Worcestershire sauce

1 teaspoon kosher salt

1 teaspoon black pepper

1   Clean and rinse the crane breasts. Place into a resealable plastic bag.

2   Pour the olive oil, red wine vinegar, soy sauce, parsley, Worcestershire sauce, salt, and pepper into the bag and combine. Add the crane breasts and mix until evenly coated.

3   Place the bag into the refrigerator for 4–48 hours.

4   Preheat your pellet grill or traditional grill to 250°F (120°C). If using a traditional grill, only turn on one side to allow for indirect heat cooking.

5   Remove the crane from the marinade and season both sides with salt and pepper.

6   Set the marinated crane breast directly onto the grill grate. (Use the indirect heat side for traditional grill.) Cook until the internal temperature reads 125°F (52°C). This will take around 40 minutes depending on the size of the crane breast. Check the temperature around the 30-minute mark to make sure you don't overcook it. Once the crane breast reaches temperature, remove from the grill, set onto a plate, and tent with foil.

7   Turn the grill up to full or high and let it come to temperature while the meat rests.

8   Once the grill has come to temperature, sear the crane breasts for 2 minutes per side or until you get the desired char.

9   Remove from the grill and let rest again for 5 minutes before slicing.

VENISON STEAKS WITH SPICY CHIMICHURRI

Chimichurri is a South American sauce that has a fresh, herbaceous flavor. My recipe has a kick of spice as well. The fresh herbs, spices, and vinegar making it zesty, spicy, and fragrant. It pairs perfectly with grilled red meats, like drizzled over this venison backstrap steak. I highly recommend cooking your venison steaks to medium-rare to make sure they are not too tough.

Yield: 4 servings

1 venison backstrap, about
1½–2 pounds (680 to 900 g), whole

2 tablespoons (28 ml) extra-virgin olive oil

1 tablespoon (14 g) kosher salt

1 teaspoon chili powder

1 teaspoon onion powder

SPICY CHIMICHURRI

½ cup (30 g) fresh parsley, packed

½ cup (8 g) fresh cilantro, packed

¼ small red onion, chopped

2 jalapeños, seeded and chopped

3 garlic cloves

1 tablespoon (3 g) dried oregano

1 teaspoon kosher salt

½ teaspoon black pepper

½ cup (120 ml) extra-virgin olive oil

⅓ cup (80 ml) red wine vinegar

½ teaspoon crushed red pepper

1 About an hour before cooking, remove the backstrap from the refrigerator and set on a plate. This allows it to come up to room temperature slightly. Then, about 30 minutes before grilling, make the chimichurri. Preheat the grill to medium-high, about 450°F (230°C), before starting or partway through making the chimichurri, so it is ready to go when you are.

2 To make the chimichurri, combine the parsley, cilantro, red onion, jalapeño, garlic, oregano, salt, and pepper into a food processor. Pulse for 5–10 seconds to combine. Slowly add olive oil and red wine vinegar until evenly blended. Add the crushed red pepper. If you do not have a food processor, finely dice the parsley, cilantro, red onion, and garlic, and then whisk them with the rest of the ingredients. Set aside.

3 Pat the venison dry with a paper towel. Season all sides with olive oil and spices.

4 Place the venison on the preheated grill. Grill until medium-rare or to your desired temperature, flipping the steaks halfway through cooking. I've found medium-rare will usually take about 7–10 minutes per side. Depending on the exact size of your steak, this could take more or less time. Use a temperature probe to monitor the temperature.

5 When the venison is finished cooking, transfer to a plate or serving dish and cover with foil. Allow the venison to rest for 5 minutes.

6 Slice the venison into strips, drizzle with the chimichurri, and serve.

TEMPERATURE GUIDE FOR VENISON STEAKS

Rare: 120–125°F (49 to 52°C); medium-rare: 125–130°F (52 to 54°C); medium: 130–140°F (54°C to 60°C); medium-well: 140–150°F (60 to 66°C); and well-done: 150°F+ (66°C +)

REVERSE-SEARED VENISON BACKSTRAP WITH HERB BUTTER

I'll never forget the first time I reverse-seared a steak. The recipe was very similar to this one, and the flavors were epic to say the least. The process is exactly as it sounds: it flips the traditional way to cook thick steaks. You start off at a low temperature, allow the steak to cook a bit, and then give it a quick sear at very high heat on both sides. The herb butter is melt-in-your-mouth delicious (literally!). It's the perfect kiss of herb and garlic flavors over top a perfectly cooked steak.

Yield: 4–5 servings

2 teaspoons minced garlic

2 tablespoons (weight will vary) finely chopped fresh herbs (thyme, parsley, and rosemary)

1 stick (½ cup, or 112 g) butter, softened

1–2 pounds (455 to 900 g) venison backstrap, whole

2 teaspoons salt

1 teaspoon black pepper

1 tablespoon (15 ml) extra-virgin olive oil

1 Mix the garlic and herbs into the softened butter until smooth. Place the mixture onto a sheet of wax paper and roll into a log about 1½ inch (3.8 cm) in diameter and refrigerate.

2 Pat the venison backstrap dry with paper towels. Season with salt and pepper on all sides. Rub into the meat using your hands and 1 tablespoon (15 ml) of olive oil.

3 Preheat your smoker or grill to 250°F (120°C). If using a grill, only turn on one side to allow for indirect heat cooking.

4 Set the venison backstrap into the smoker onto the grill grate. (Use the indirect heat side for traditional grill.) Cook until the internal temperature reads 125°F (66°C). This will take around 40 minutes. Check the temperature around the 30-minute mark to make sure you don't overcook the meat. Once the backstrap reaches temperature, remove from the grill and set onto a plate.

5 Turn the grill up to full or high and let it come to temperature while the steaks rest.

6 Once the grill has come to temperature, sear the backstrap for 45 seconds to 1 minute per side.

7 Remove the venison from the grill and set to let rest for 5 minutes.

8 Slice into steaks. Add at least two pats of the garlic and herb butter to each steak and let them melt over the meat.

MARINATED GRILLED VENISON TENDERLOIN

There are four main components to any good marinade: cooking oil, salt, an acid, and flavoring. The oil holds all of the ingredients together and adds moisture to the meat. Salt tenderizes the meat by drawing water out. It also plays a flavor-enhancing role. The acid helps tenderize the meat and adds balance to any fat. (The acid can be in many forms such as vinegar, lemon juice, or wine.) Lastly, the flavor: this is the fun part. There aren't many rules when it comes to the flavor, and it's always fun to try new combinations. See page 144 and choose your own adventure!

Yield: 4 servings

1 pound (455 g) venison tenderloin, whole

1 recipe from My Favorite Marinades sidebar (see page 144)

1 Remove all visible fat and most of the silver skin from the venison.

2 Mix together all the marinade ingredients. Add the tenderloin to the marinade and refrigerate, covered, for 1–2 hours.

3 Preheat the grill to medium-high heat, about 450°F (230°C). Remove the meat from marinade and place it onto a plate to rest for 20–30 minutes. Discard any remaining marinade.

4 Sear over direct heat on both sides, approximately 5 minutes per side for medium-rare. Depending on the exact size of your tenderloin, this could take more or less time. Use a temperature probe to monitor the temperature.

5 When your meat is grilled to your liking, remove it from the heat.

6 Let it rest for 10 minutes before slicing and serving.

MY FAVORITE MARINADES

THE GO-TO MARINADE

¼ cup (60 ml) extra-virgin olive oil

¼ cup (60 ml) balsamic vinegar

¼ cup (60 ml) low-sodium soy sauce

2 teaspoons Dijon mustard

2 tablespoons (28 ml) Worcestershire sauce

2 teaspoons minced garlic

¼ teaspoon salt

¼ teaspoon black pepper

UMAMI MARINADE

⅓ cup (80 ml) freshly squeezed lemon juice

⅓ cup (80 ml) low-sodium soy sauce

¼ cup (60 ml) extra-virgin olive oil

¼ cup (60 ml) Worcestershire sauce

1 tablespoon (1 g) dried parsley

1 tablespoon (7 g) onion powder

1 tablespoon (3 g) dried basil

1 teaspoon garlic salt

1 teaspoon black pepper

HONEY GINGER MARINADE

2 garlic cloves, thinly sliced

1 tablespoon (15 ml) sesame oil

¼ cup (60 ml) low-sodium soy sauce

1 teaspoon honey

1 teaspoon thinly sliced fresh ginger

¼ teaspoon salt

¼ teaspoon black pepper

RED WINE MARINADE

¼ cup (60 ml) extra-virgin olive oil

¼ cup (60 ml) red wine vinegar

¼ cup (60 ml) low-sodium soy sauce

¼ cup (15 g) chopped fresh parsley

1 teaspoon kosher salt

1 teaspoon black pepper

DEER HUNTING

I started out deer hunting with my father in the game lands of Pennsylvania. I never watched hunting on TV although plenty of friends and family told me their hunting stories. In those early days, my dad and I didn't have all that much success, but I was happy to be there, even if my frozen face would seem to tell a different story!

As I got older, our hunts were more productive, and I enjoyed them all the more. Eventually, I picked up a bow. The bow turned into a big obsession—eventually I had a practice area and worked at it just about every day. That obsession lasts to this day: there is a different type of adrenaline when you're drawing back on your bow and a big buck is less than 20 yards (18 m) away. Those heart-pounding, unforgettable moments are the reason the early mornings and hard work are all worth it in the end.

VENISON SMASH BURGERS

What is a smash burger? The name gives it away. It is derived from the method of pressing or smashing meat onto a hot griddle, giving you a perfectly browned crust to your burger. This recipe is so easy, you simply cannot mess it up if you follow the instructions! Just make sure to blend the ground pork with the venison; otherwise, your burgers won't have quite enough fat. And keep that ground meat cold until right before you cook it.

Yield: 2 double-decker burgers

1 pound (455 g) ground venison

½ pound (225 g) ground pork

1 teaspoon balsamic vinegar

½ teaspoon Worcestershire sauce

1 teaspoon garlic powder

½ teaspoon onion powder

1 tablespoon (4 g) chopped fresh parsley

1 teaspoon salt

½ teaspoon black pepper

4 slices cheddar cheese

2 burger buns, toasted

2 cups (144 g) iceberg lettuce, shredded

1 large tomato, sliced

½ red onion, sliced into thin rings

Parchment paper, for cooking

1. Mix the ground venison, ground pork, balsamic vinegar, Worcestershire sauce, garlic powder, onion powder, parsley, salt, and pepper into a large bowl.

2. Divide into four even portions, about 4 ounces (115 g) each. Loosely roll them into balls and then cover and refrigerate while preparing the remaining ingredients for toppings and preheating the griddle or pan. The meat must be cold when it hits the griddle or pan!

3. Preheat your griddle to medium-high heat or get a large cast-iron skillet greased and heating to medium-high.

4. Place the four burger balls onto the hot griddle or skillet. Working quickly, place parchment paper over the meat and firmly smash straight down into a thin patty. Remove the parchment paper. Cook 2 minutes on the first side. They should look seared, and juices should start to come to the surface.

5. Scrape under the burger and flip. Cook for another minute. Top the patties with a slice of cheddar cheese.

6. Serve two patties per toasted bun and add lettuce, sliced tomato, sliced red onion, and condiments as desired.

CHIPOTLE VENISON STEAK KABOBS

These juicy kabobs feature chunks of venison that are marinated in chipotle peppers, garlic, and lime juice. The venison chunks are threaded onto kabobs with bell peppers and onions and grilled until they have the perfect char on the outside and are tender inside. This recipe makes for an easy handheld meal that's perfect for summer parties.

Yield: 8–10 skewers

2½ pounds (1.1 kg) venison steak (backstrap or roast)

1 can (7 ounces, or 200 g) chipotle peppers in adobo sauce

1 tablespoon (10 g) minced garlic

Juice of 1 lime

1 teaspoon black pepper

1 green bell pepper, seeded and diced into 2-inch (5 cm) pieces

1 red bell pepper, seeded and diced into 2-inch (5 cm) pieces

1 onion, diced into 2-inch (5 cm) pieces

10 metal or wooden skewers, for cooking

1 If you're not using metal skewers, soak at least 10 wooden skewers in water for half an hour. This will prevent them from burning when cooking.

2 Cut the venison into 2- to 3-inch (5 to 7.5 cm) pieces. Place into a bowl with a lid or resealable bag.

3 Place the chipotle peppers in adobo, garlic, lime juice, and pepper into the bag. Mix until evenly distributed. Place in the refrigerator to marinate for 30 minutes.

4 Preheat the grill to high heat.

5 Get out 8–10 skewers. If using wooden skewers, be sure to soak them in water 30 minutes before grilling so they don't burn. Thread the venison pieces, bell peppers, and onion onto the skewers, spaced evenly.

6 Grill the skewers for a total of 6 minutes. Use tongs to turn the skewers frequently to ensure that all sides get in contact with the heat.

7 Remove the skewers from the grill and serve immediately.

APRICOT-DIJON GLAZED WILD TURKEY

This recipe is bursting with flavor! With this dish, you get the sweet mellow tones of apricot and a subtle tang from the Dijon mustard. Apricot jam and Dijon mustard meld together perfectly while you grill the turkey, forming the most delicious glazed wild game dinner. It takes only minutes to make and involves little work, making it great for weeknights or busy weekends.

Yield: 4—6 servings

Cooking oil or nonstick cooking spray, for coating grill

1 boneless, skinless wild turkey breast, approximately 2 pounds (900 g)

1 tablespoon (15 ml) extra-virgin olive oil

½ teaspoon salt

¼ teaspoon black pepper

½ cup (160 g) apricot jam

1 tablespoon (15 ml) apple cider vinegar

1 tablespoon (15 g) Dijon mustard

1 tablespoon (15 ml) low-sodium soy sauce

2 garlic cloves, minced

1 Heat half of a grill to medium-high for indirect grilling. Lightly coat the grill grates with cooking oil or nonstick cooking spray.

2 Clean and rinse the wild turkey breast. Pat dry with paper towels. Cover with plastic wrap and pound into even thickness using a meat mallet. Brush with olive oil and season with the salt and pepper on both sides. Place into a resealable plastic bag.

3 In a medium-sized bowl, stir together apricot jam, apple cider vinegar, Dijon mustard, soy sauce, and garlic. Pour ¾ of the marinade over the wild turkey breast and refrigerate for 1 hour. Reserve ¼ cup (60 ml) of the marinade in a separate container and store in the refrigerator.

4 Grill over indirect heat for 20 minutes, turning halfway. Brush with the reserved apricot-mustard mixture and grill an additional 15—20 minutes or until internal temperature registers 165°F (74°C) on an instant-read thermometer.

5 Slice and serve.

THAI CHILI GRILLED TURKEY LETTUCE CUPS

This dish is on the healthier side, but that doesn't mean it's light on flavor. The wild turkey breast is marinated in garlic, lime juice, chili sauce, soy sauce, ginger, and a blend of seasonings. It's grilled over indirect heat to help it stay nice and juicy. It's the star of these fresh lettuce cups. Mine are filled with cilantro, shredded carrots, red onions, and a drizzle of the Thai chili mayo for a crisp and refreshing treat. But you can also switch up the fillings to suit your taste or even add rice or thin rice noodles to your cups if you want them to be a little more filling.

Yield: 8 servings

1 boneless, skinless wild turkey breast, approximately 2 pounds (900 g)

1 teaspoon salt

1 teaspoon chili powder

1 teaspoon ground cumin

1 teaspoon paprika

2 garlic cloves, minced

2 tablespoons (28 ml) extra-virgin olive oil

Juice and zest of 2 limes

½ cup (113 g) Thai chili sauce

¼ cup (60 ml) low-sodium soy sauce

2 teaspoons freshly grated ginger

1 head bibb lettuce, leaves separated (You'll want at least 8–10 good-sized leaves for this recipe.)

1 carrot, shredded, for garnish

1 red onion, julienned, for garnish

1 tablespoon (8 g) roughly chopped fresh cilantro, for garnish

THAI CHILI MAYO

¾ cup (175 g) mayonnaise

2 tablespoons (28 g) Thai chili sauce

1 tablespoon (15 ml) freshly squeezed lime juice

1   Clean and rinse the wild turkey breast. Pat dry with a paper towel and then season with salt, chili powder, cumin, and paprika. Place into a resealable plastic bag.

2   In a small bowl, combine the garlic, olive oil, lime juice and zest, chili sauce, soy sauce, and ginger. Mix until all the ingredients are combined. Pour half of the marinade over the turkey. Refrigerate for at least 1 hour. Reserve the rest of the marinade in a separate container in the refrigerator for later.

3   Grill the turkey, covered, over indirect medium heat until the internal temperature reaches 165°F (74°C). This can take around 40 minutes depending on the size of your turkey breasts.

4   While the turkey breast is cooking, mix all the ingredients for the Thai chili mayo in a small bowl and set aside in the refrigerator.

5   Once the turkey is cooked, remove from the grill and let rest for about 5 minutes. Cut into small bite-size pieces, pour the reserved marinade over top, and divide into about eight lettuce leaves. (Depending on your head of lettuce, you may be able to fill a few more.)

6   Garnish the lettuce cups with shredded carrot, red onion, and chopped fresh cilantro. Serve drizzled with the Thai chili mayo.

JAMAICAN JERK PHEASANT

This dish is my take on an island classic. The combination of scotch bonnet peppers, soy sauce, lime, thyme, allspice, and nutmeg create the foundation for the Jamaican jerk seasoning. There are hints of salty, sweet, and a lot of spicy flavors in this dish. While the Scotch bonnet peppers are a signature taste in this recipe, if you can't find them, this is still quite delicious with a substitute pepper like Serrano.

Yield: 4 servings

4 boneless, skinless pheasant breasts, approximately 4–5 ounces (115 to 140 g) each

3 green onions, chopped

4 garlic cloves, chopped

1 onion, chopped

4 scotch bonnet peppers, stemmed and seeded, or serrano peppers

¼ cup (60 ml) freshly squeezed lime juice

2 tablespoons (28 ml) low-sodium soy sauce

3 tablespoons (45 ml) extra-virgin olive oil

1 tablespoon (15 g) packed brown sugar

1 tablespoon (18 g) salt

1 tablespoon (2 g) fresh thyme

1 teaspoon ground allspice

½ teaspoon nutmeg

½ teaspoon black pepper

1 Add the pheasant to a resealable plastic bag.

2 In a food processor, add the green onions, garlic, onion, scotch bonnet peppers, lime juice, soy sauce, olive oil, brown sugar, salt, thyme, allspice, nutmeg, and pepper and purée until smooth.

3 Add the marinade to the bag with the pheasant breast and place in the refrigerator to marinate for at least 1 hour.

4 Preheat the grill to medium-high heat.

5 Grill on each side for 5–7 minutes, depending on the size of the breast, until completely cooked through.

6 Remove from the grill and serve immediately.

HONEY GARLIC WILD TURKEY ON A STICK

When I'm at the fair, I love getting chicken on a stick, so of course, I had to make a wild game version with my own spin. While honey and garlic are the standout flavors, you also get hits of salt and umami flavors from the soy sauce, a fresh aroma from the ginger, and a touch of tartness from the apple cider vinegar. Your family will love this for dinner served with a bed of rice, but it's also great as an appetizer or as part of a spread.

Yield: 6–8 skewers

¼ cup (60 ml) low-sodium soy sauce

1 tablespoon (15 ml) sesame oil

1 tablespoon (15 ml) apple cider vinegar

4 tablespoons (80 g) honey

2 garlic cloves, minced

1 teaspoon minced fresh ginger

1 tablespoon (8 g) cornstarch

1 boneless, skinless wild turkey breast, approximately 2 pounds (900 g), cut into strips 1-inch (2.5 cm) long

6–8 skewers

Nonstick cooking spray, for coating grill

1 Whisk together the soy sauce, sesame oil, apple cider vinegar, honey, garlic, and ginger into a small bowl.

2 Slowly add the cornstarch to thicken the sauce.

3 Place the turkey strips into a resealable bag or a lidded container. Pour the marinade over top, reserving some in a separate container in the refrigerator for basting. Marinate in the refrigerator for at least 1 hour.

4 Halfway through marinating, soak your wooden skewers in water for at least half an hour. You can skip this step if you're using metal skewers.

5 Thread the turkey strips onto the skewers.

6 Once you're ready to cook, preheat your grill to medium-high heat. Lightly coat the grill grates with nonstick cooking spray to prevent sticking.

7 Once the grill is preheated, place the turkey skewers on the grill and cook until well browned on one side, 5–7 minutes. Turn and baste with the reserved marinade. Grill for another 5–7 minutes. Turn and baste again. The internal temperature should be 165°F (74°C), and the wild turkey should be caramelized on the outside.

8 Remove from the heat and let the meat rest for 5 minutes before slicing and serving.

VENISON WITH MUSTARD SAUCE

In this recipe, the venison steaks are kept simple. A little extra-virgin olive oil and salt and black pepper go a long way. I've found this is often the best approach when it's the sauce that will elevate the meat to another level. If you season the meat aggressively, it will often compete too much with the sauce. This delicious mustard sauce is a combination of shallots, olive oil, two different mustards, heavy cream, and tarragon. It's designed to stand up to the strong flavors of a grilled venison steak.

Yield: 2 servings

1½ pounds (680 g) venison steak about 1-inch (2.5 cm) thick

1 tablespoon (15 ml) extra-virgin olive oil

1 teaspoon salt

½ teaspoon black pepper

Nonstick cooking spray, for coating grill

MUSTARD SAUCE

1 tablespoon (15 ml) extra-virgin olive oil

1 shallot, finely diced

2 tablespoons (28 ml) brandy

1¼ cups (295 ml) heavy cream

2 tablespoons (30 g) Dijon mustard

1 tablespoon (15 g) whole-grain mustard

1 tablespoon (4 g) chopped tarragon

¼ teaspoon salt

¼ teaspoon black pepper

1 Prepare the mustard sauce: Add olive oil to a medium skillet set over medium-low heat. Add the shallots and cook for 2–3 minutes or until shallots have softened. Add the brandy and stir for 2–3 minutes or until the liquor evaporates. Add the heavy cream, both mustards, tarragon, and salt and pepper to the pan. Reduce the heat to low and simmer for 5–6 minutes. The sauce should start to thicken.

2 Lightly coat the grill grates with nonstick cooking spray and heat the grill to 500°F (250°C).

3 Pat the venison dry with paper towels and then rub both sides of the steak with olive oil, salt, and pepper.

4 Lay the steak on the preheated grill. Use tongs to pick up the steak and move it 90 degrees on the grill, which will give you the crosshatch grill marks. Grill for another 2 minutes on the same side.

5 Flip the steak and grill using the same method as the first side. Cook until medium-rare (145°F [63°C]), approximately 4 minutes. Use a meat thermometer to monitor the temperature.

6 Move the steak to a plate and let it rest for at least 5 minutes.

7 Slice the meat, pour the mustard sauce over top, and serve.

GRILLED VENISON STEAK DIANE

The traditional recipe for "Steak Diane" was a popular dish in the 1950s and 1960s that consisted of a pan-fried steak in a cream sauce that was often flambéed using cognac. Yes, it's a dish that was not made on the grill, but my goal here was to fuse the best flavors from decades past with the spirit of getting outdoors and grilling.

Yield: 2 servings

½ pound (225 g) venison backstrap, cut into steaks ¼- to ½-inch (6 to 13 mm) thick

¼ teaspoon salt

¼ teaspoon black pepper

2 tablespoons (28 g) butter

3 tablespoons (45 ml) extra-virgin olive oil

1 large shallot, julienned

2 tablespoons (28 ml) Worcestershire sauce

2 garlic cloves, diced

8 ounces (225 g) cremini mushrooms, sliced

1 teaspoon Dijon mustard

¼ cup (60 ml) cognac

½ cup (120 ml) beef broth

¼ cup (60 ml) heavy cream

2 tablespoons (8 g) chopped fresh parsley, for garnish

1 Place a large cast-iron skillet onto your grill and preheat the grill to medium-high heat, approximately 450°F (230°C).

2 Pat the venison steaks dry with paper towels. Sprinkle salt and pepper on both sides of the steak and set aside at room temperature for 15–30 minutes.

3 Once the grill is preheated and the cast-iron skillet is hot, add the butter to the pan. Be careful not to touch the skillet with your bare hands.

4 Once the butter is melted and sizzling, sear the steaks for about 1 minute per side. Remove from the pan and place onto a plate. Cover with foil.

5 In the hot cast-iron skillet, add the olive oil. Then add the shallots and cook for 1–2 minutes until they start to become translucent, stirring often. Mix in the Worcestershire sauce, garlic, and mushrooms. Cook for another 1–2 minutes, stirring often. Keep an eye on the temperature of your grill as you cook; cover the grill often if necessary to retain temperature.

6 Stir in the Dijon mustard and mix well.

7 Add the cognac, mix in, and cook until almost evaporated.

8 Stir in the beef broth and cook for 2–3 minutes. The sauce should start to thicken.

9 Stir in the heavy cream and cook for 2 minutes. Add the steaks back in and spoon the sauce and mushrooms over top.

10 Garnish with chopped fresh parsley and serve.

VENISON PHILLY CHEESESTEAKS

Growing up less than an hour from Philadelphia, you could say I've had my fair share of Philly Cheesesteaks. Now, the cheesesteaks I grew up eating were composed of thinly sliced beef, loaded with yellow cheese sauce, and placed on a good-quality hoagie roll. This recipe remixes the classic for a delicious sandwich all its own. Venison backstrap is what I like to swap in—you'll find it brings an earthier and richer taste than beef. Due partly to the flavor of the venison, I also recommend going with something like provolone. I find it just marries better than the cheese sauce. When it comes to toppings, for the classic Philly cheesesteak, you could take or leave the onions and that was about it. These days, people now add bell peppers, and mushrooms, or serve them hoagie-style with onions, tomato, and lettuce. I like onions and peppers, so that's what you'll see here. But of course, do whatever calls to you or that you think goes best with venison.

Yield: 4 servings

1 pound (455 g) venison backstrap, sliced thin

1 tablespoon (15 g) Dijon mustard

1 tablespoon (15 ml) extra-virgin olive oil

2 tablespoons (28 ml) balsamic vinegar

1 teaspoon onion powder

1 teaspoon dried thyme

1 teaspoon minced garlic

2 tablespoons (28 g) butter, divided

1 large onion, julienned

2 green bell peppers, seeded and julienned (optional)

½ teaspoon salt

¼ teaspoon black pepper

6 slices provolone cheese

1 French baguette, toasted and cut into 4 buns, or hoagie rolls

1 In a large bowl or resealable bag, combine the sliced backstrap, Dijon mustard, olive oil, balsamic vinegar, onion powder, thyme, and garlic. Marinate the venison the in refrigerator for 1 hour.

2 Heat the griddle over medium-high heat. Melt 1 tablespoon (14 g) of the butter on the griddle. Add the onion and bell peppers. Cook until just tender. Move to the side of the griddle on low heat to keep warm.

3 Melt the other tablespoon (14 g) of the butter and then add the backstrap pieces and salt and pepper and cook until no longer pink and lightly browned, approximately 5 minutes.

4 Mix the vegetables and venison together and assemble into four portion sizes. Top with provolone cheese and cover with the griddle lid to melt.

5 Once melted, place onto the toasted baguette and serve.

SIMPLE RAMEN DUCK STIR-FRY

Ready in no time at all, this super delicious weeknight dinner will get the big thumbs-up from your family. Duck meat brings a meatier and richer taste to stir-fry—it is hard to put into words just how good it is, but if you've enjoyed duck before, you know what I mean. The delicious flavor of duck still stands out in this recipe next to the ginger, garlic, and apricot aromas. If you want to make this recipe even easier, you can swap out store-bought stir-fry sauce and have dinner in minutes.

Yield: 4–6 servings

Cooking oil, for coating griddle

4–6 boneless, skinless duck breasts, approximately 3 ounces (85 g) each, cut into thin strips

2 tablespoons (28 g) butter

2 green bell peppers, seeded and julienned

½ cup (55 g) shredded carrots

½ onion, julienned

2 packages (3 ounces, or 85 g each) cooked ramen noodles (discard flavor packet)

MARINADE

½ cup (120 ml) low-sodium soy sauce

⅓ cup (80 ml) low-sodium, low-sugar, seasoned rice vinegar

⅓ cup (107 g) apricot preserves

1 tablespoon (15 g) light brown sugar

3 tablespoons (30 g) minced garlic

1 tablespoon (6 g) minced fresh ginger

STIR-FRY SAUCE

⅓ cup (80 ml) low-sodium soy sauce

¼ cup (60 ml) water

2 tablespoons (28 ml) rice vinegar

2 teaspoons (28 ml) sesame oil

1 tablespoon (20 g) honey

3 garlic cloves, minced

1-inch (2.5 cm) knob fresh ginger, minced

½ teaspoon crushed red pepper

1 Combine all the marinade ingredients in a bowl and whisk together. Add the duck breast strips, mix to combine, and then marinate for at least 4 hours in the refrigerator.

2 Combine the stir-fry sauce ingredients in a medium-sized bowl. Stir and set aside.

3 Heat the cooking oil on a griddle or in a pan over medium heat.

4 Add the duck strips and sauté for 2 minutes, stirring often. Remove from the heat.

5 Add the butter and vegetables and the stir-fry sauce to the same pan. Sauté for 5 minutes. The vegetables should start to look tender.

6 Add the duck back to the pan and cook to your desired doneness, about 3–5 minutes. The duck should be browned but still juicy and tender. Stir in the cooked ramen noodles until they are mixed well with the other ingredients and warmed through.

7 When ready, serve and enjoy!

VENISON SLOPPY JOE STUFFED GRILLED CHEESE

This combines two childhood favorites all in one delicious sandwich. I love making this recipe on a griddle as you can cook the venison and veggies like an expert short-order chef! The venison and veggies then get smothered with sloppy joe sauce, topped with cheese, and placed between two hearty pieces of Texas toast. It's an epic sandwich, but you can also stop after you combine the sauce and venison and go your own way. It works well served over rice or as part of a chili mac as well (just add shredded cheese and some raw diced onion to garnish).

Yield: 4 sandwiches

2 tablespoons (28 g) butter, softened

2 tablespoons (28 g) mayonnaise

8 slices Texas toast

1 tablespoon (14 g) butter

1 tablespoon (15 ml) extra-virgin olive oil

1 pound (455 g) ground venison

½ medium onion, diced

1 green bell pepper, seeded and diced

2 cups (225 g) shredded cheddar cheese

SLOPPY JOE SAUCE

1 tablespoon (15 ml) Worcestershire sauce

⅔ cup (160 g) ketchup

1 teaspoon chili powder

½ teaspoon paprika

½ teaspoon salt

¼ teaspoon black pepper

1 In a medium-sized bowl, combine all the sloppy joe sauce ingredients. Mix well and set aside.

2 Mix the butter and mayo in a small bowl. Use a butter knife to spread the butter mixture on one side of each of the Texas toast pieces.

3 Preheat the griddle to medium-high heat and melt the butter with the olive oil. Add the ground venison and brown for 3–4 minutes, chopping up the meat with a spatula as it cooks.

4 Add the onion and bell pepper and cook for an additional 3 minutes.

5 Pour the sloppy joe sauce over the venison mixture. Cook for 5 minutes, mixing often. Move to one side of the griddle and reduce the heat to medium-low.

6 Place four slices of the Texas toast onto the griddle, butter-side down. Top each with ¼ of the cheddar cheese and then top with approximately ½ cup (120 ml) of the sloppy joe mix. Place another piece of Texas toast on top of each one, butter-side up. Cook until the bottom slice is starting to brown and flip the whole sandwich. Cover with a melting dome and allow the cheese to melt.

7 Once the cheese has melted, remove from the griddle and serve.

VENISON BIRRIA TACOS

Birria is a flavor-packed combination of savory, sweet, earthy, smoky, and spicy seasonings. It is a traditional Mexican dish that is built around delicious stewed meat, with the signature flavor of guajillo chiles. The meat goes in the tortillas, which are then filled with cheese and fried on a hot griddle. The crisp tacos are served with the braising liquid, called consommé. Don't skip the lime juice—it's key!

Yield: 6–8 servings

4 dried guajillo chiles, seeds and stems removed

3–4 pounds (1.4 to 1.8 kg) venison roast

1 tablespoon (18 g) salt

1 teaspoon black pepper

2 tablespoons (28 ml) extra-virgin olive oil

2 chipotle peppers in adobo

1 cup (235 ml) water

½ cup (120 g) crushed tomatoes

1 onion, chopped

4 garlic cloves, minced

2 bay leaves

2 teaspoons dried Mexican oregano

½ teaspoon dried thyme

1 teaspoon salt

1 teaspoon black pepper

Pinch of ground cinnamon

Pinch of ground cloves

1 tablespoon (15 cm) apple cider vinegar

3 cups (700 ml) beef broth

Cooking oil or nonstick cooking spray, for coating griddle

TACOS

12 corn tortillas (4 inches, or 10 cm)

2 cups (230 g) shredded Monterey Jack cheese

1–2 limes, cut into wedges

1 bunch fresh finely chopped cilantro, for garnish

½ red onion, finely diced, for garnish

1 Remove the seeds and stems from the guajillo chiles. Add the guajillo chiles to a medium pot with water and bring to a boil. Once boiling, cover and then remove from heat. Soak your dried guajillo chiles for 15 minutes and then strain off the liquid.

2 While the chiles are soaking, take the venison roast and season with salt and pepper on all sides. In a large pan, heat the olive oil over medium-high heat and brown the roast on all sides, 2–3 minutes per side.

3 In a small blender, add the guajillo chiles, chipotle peppers, and 1 cup (235 ml) of water. Blend for 30 seconds or until the peppers are chopped up nicely.

4 Add the venison roast to a large (7 quart [6.6 L] or more) slow cooker. Pour the blended peppers over top. Add the crushed tomatoes, onion, garlic, bay leaves, Mexican oregano, thyme, salt, pepper, cinnamon, and cloves. Pour the apple cider vinegar and beef broth over top. Cover and cook on high for 4–6 hours.

5 Once the roast is finished cooking, use a ladle to spoon off any liquid from the top of the slow cooker, trying not to get anything but the liquid. Reserve for cooking the tortillas. Remove the cooked meat from the pot and shred completely. Reserve the cooking liquid in the slow cooker as a side dish, the consommé, for the tacos to be dipped into.

6 Heat your griddle over medium heat. Lightly coat with nonstick cooking spray or pour a small amount of cooking oil over the top of the griddle. Dip a tortilla into the reserved liquid from the slow cooker and place onto the griddle. Repeat this step and fill the griddle with as many tortillas as will fit without overlapping. Spoon some of the shredded meat into the tortilla, about 1–2 tongs' worth. Top with Monterey Jack cheese and then fold tightly into a taco. Fry for 1–2 minutes, carefully flip, and then fry the other side for 1–2 minutes more until the shells are crisp and the cheese is melted.

7 Squeeze lime juice over the tacos. Garnish with chopped fresh cilantro and diced red onion. Serve with the consommé for dipping.

BOURBON WILD TURKEY

The recipe includes soy sauce, brown sugar, and ginger, but of course it's the bourbon whiskey that will have folks talking. (And if you pick a certain brand, then it really goes with the turkey, if you know what I mean!). Sautéed on a hot griddle, the alcohol will cook off but the flavor will stick around. Mixed with bell peppers and onions, it's a perfectly easy weeknight dinner.

Yield: 4–6 servings

1 large boneless, skinless wild turkey breast, approximately 2½–3 pounds (1.1 to 1.4 kg)

3 tablespoons (24 g) cornstarch, divided

½ teaspoon salt

¼ teaspoon black pepper

¼ cup (60 ml) bourbon

⅔ cup (160 ml) low-sodium soy sauce

1 tablespoon (8 g) cornstarch

3 tablespoons (45 ml) water

2 tablespoons (28 ml) apple cider vinegar

½ cup (115 g) packed light brown sugar

1 teaspoon ground ginger

½ teaspoon crushed red pepper

2 tablespoons (28 ml) cooking oil

2 garlic cloves, minced

1 yellow onion, large diced

2 green bell pepper, seeded and large diced

1 Cut the wild turkey into 1-inch (2.5 cm) pieces. In a large bowl, toss the turkey pieces with 2 tablespoons (16 g) of the cornstarch, salt, and pepper.

2 Prepare the bourbon sauce by mixing the bourbon, soy sauce, 1 tablespoon (8 g) of cornstarch dissolved in 3 tablespoons (45 ml) of cold water, apple cider vinegar, brown sugar, ginger, and crushed red pepper. Stir to incorporate all the ingredients and set aside.

3 Preheat griddle to medium-high. Add 2 tablespoons (28 ml) of cooking oil. Once the oil is hot, add the turkey pieces and cook for 6–8 minutes, flipping halfway. The turkey will not be fully cooked at this point. Remove from the griddle and set aside.

4 Add the garlic and cook until just fragrant, 30 seconds or less.

5 Add the onion and bell peppers. Sauté for approximately 3 minutes, stirring often.

6 Add the turkey back to the pan and reduce the heat to low. Add the sauce in three to four batches. Wait a few minutes in between to allow the sauce to reduce and thicken.

7 Once the sauce has thickened, check the temperature of the wild turkey pieces with an internal thermometer. Continue sautéing until the temperature reaches 165°F (74°C).

8 Serve over white rice.

VENISON CRUNCHY WRAPS

Crunch those cravings with this delicious wild game remix of a fast-food favorite. It's a super-fun recipe to make on your griddle. You start by browning the ground venison on the griddle and smothering it in taco seasoning. Then, you deftly assemble the wrap by layering two different types of cheese, tomato, shredded lettuce, sour cream, and the crunchy tostada, wrapping it all in another tortilla and toasting it to perfection. Order up!

Yield: 6 servings

Cooking oil, for coating griddle

1 pound (455 g) ground venison

1 package (1 ounce, or 28 g) taco seasoning mix

6 burrito-sized soft flour tortillas

1 jar (15 ounces, or 425 g) nacho cheese

1 tomato, diced

2 cups (144 g) shredded lettuce

6 tostadas

8 ounces (225 g) sour cream

2 cups (225 g) shredded Mexican-style cheese blend

6 fajita-sized soft flour tortillas

1   Preheat the griddle to medium heat and coat with cooking oil. Once hot, place ground venison onto the griddle and cook until browned, crumbling the meat into small pieces as it cooks.

2   Once the venison is browned, add the taco seasoning and mix until the venison is evenly coated. Set aside to cool.

3   Lay a burrito-sized tortilla on a plate or cutting board. Spread nacho cheese onto the tortilla. Then, place a handful of diced tomato and a handful of shredded lettuce in the center of the tortilla on top of the nacho cheese.

4   Place the tostada on top of the veggies and then add a large dollop of sour cream to the center. Using the back of a spoon, spread it around the tostada.

5   Add about a ½ cup (120 ml) of the cooked venison to the wrap and then sprinkle a generous handful of Mexican-style cheese over the top. Top with a fajita-sized tortilla.

6   Fold the outer tortilla edges inward over the filling, creating a pentagon-shaped wrap.

7   Heat a lightly oiled nonstick pan on low and toast the wrap with the folded side down.

8   Toast in the pan until the tortilla browns, the cheese begins to melt, and the folded side seals itself shut. Then, flip and toast the other side.

9   Remove from the pan, slice in half if desired, and serve.

JALAPEÑO POPPER QUESADILLAS WITH WILD TURKEY

This recipe has all of the delicious flavors of a jalapeño popper stuffed between two tortillas. The griddle is perfect for this recipe as you'll use it in a couple different ways. First, you'll sear the wild turkey that gets seasoned with cayenne and cumin. Once cooked, it gets shredded and then mixed with the cheeses and jalapeños. Then, it's back to the hot griddle so you can get the tortillas perfectly crispy for the ultimate quesadilla.

Yield: 4 servings

Cooking oil or nonstick cooking spray, for coating griddle

1 large boneless, skinless wild turkey breast, approximately 2½–3 pounds (1.1 to 1.4 kg)

2 teaspoons cayenne pepper

1 teaspoon ground cumin

1 teaspoon salt

½ teaspoon black pepper

10 jalapeños, seeded and sliced

2 packages (8 ounces, or 225 g each) cream cheese, softened

4 cups (450 g) shredded cheddar cheese

8 flour tortillas

2 tablespoons (2 g) chopped fresh cilantro, for garnish

1   Preheat the griddle to medium heat and coat with cooking oil.

2   Take your turkey breast half and cut it in half again. Try to get the pieces to be as close in size as possible for even cooking. Season with cayenne, cumin, salt, and black pepper on both sides. Place on the hot griddle and cook until the temperature reaches 165°F (74°C), approximately 7 minutes per side depending on the size of the breast. Flip halfway. Remove from the griddle, set onto a plate, and tent with foil.

3   Once the turkey cools for at least 5 minutes, shred with two forks. Place into a large mixing bowl. Add the jalapeños, softened cream cheese, and cheddar cheese. Stir until mixed evenly.

4   Lightly apply cooking oil or nonstick cooking spray to the griddle.

5   Place four tortillas onto the griddle so that they don't overlap. Spread ¼ of the filling on each of the tortillas. Top with the remaining four tortillas. Cook until golden brown on both sides, approximately 3 minutes.

6   Transfer to a cutting board, slice into quarters, and garnish with chopped fresh cilantro before serving.

BLUE CHEESE VENISON BURGERS

For many people, blue cheese is an acquired taste. I'll admit, as a child, I was certainly not a fan! But since then, I've come around. I've found recipes like this one are a great way to introduce blue cheese to those who no longer "hate" it but haven't yet come around to appreciate all it can offer. The venison patty is seasoned with the flavors of garlic, onion, mustard, salt, and black pepper. These enhance the flavor, but it's a restrained amount since there's blue cheese mixed into the burger as well.

Yield: 4 burgers

4 tablespoons (55 g) butter, divided

1 yellow onion, sliced

1½ pounds (680 g) ground venison

1 cup (120 g) blue cheese, plus more for serving

1 teaspoon dry mustard

2 teaspoons garlic powder

1 teaspoon Worcestershire sauce

1 teaspoon salt

½ teaspoon black pepper

4 brioche buns

Lettuce

1 tomato, sliced

1 Preheat one side of your griddle to medium-low for the onion and the other to medium-high for the burgers.

2 Melt 2 tablespoons (28 g) of butter and then add the onion and cook on medium-low until caramelized, 15–20 minutes.

3 In a large mixing bowl, combine the ground venison, ½ cup (60 g) blue cheese, dry mustard, garlic powder, Worcestershire sauce, and salt and pepper. Mix with your hands until just combined. Form into four burger patties.

4 On the side of your griddle preheated to medium-high, melt remaining 2 tablespoons (28 g) of butter.

5 Place the patties onto the melted butter and cook for 3–4 minutes per side.

6 When burgers are almost done, toast the buns on the griddle until they are golden brown.

7 When the burgers are done and reach an internal temperature of 165°F (74°C), remove them from the griddle.

8 Place on the toasted buns and a bed of lettuce. Then, top the burger with the caramelized onions, more crumbled blue cheese, and sliced tomato.

6

BUTCHERY

VENISON BUTCHERY BASICS

One of the main benefits hunting provides is an ample supply of nutritious meat. After a successful hunt, it is important that you properly take care of the animal and process it in a timely manner. There is a lot that happens between the time the animal is shot and the time it's packaged and placed in the freezer. This chapter will help with all of the steps you need to follow for venison.

While there are different methods of processing a deer, they all follow the same principles: field dressing, skinning (removing the hide), butchery (removing the meat), and storage (packaging the meat and keeping it at the proper temperature until ready to use).

Field Dressing

The first step after killing your deer is to legally tag and follow state guidelines for reporting your harvest. After that, you can start to field dress it. Field dressing, or "gutting," refers to removing all of the internal organs from the deer. It is important to field dress your deer as soon as you can to help to cool the meat and prevent spoiling or contamination. This applies to all temperatures; even during cold months it is important to field dress quickly.

1. To field dress your deer, it's best to find an area with a slight slope. Position the deer belly up with its legs in the air and back end toward the downward end of the slope.
2. Using a sharp knife, cut and make a small slit midway up the belly. At this point, I only like to cut the hide. Then, I make another cut into the skin with the blade facing upward to ensure that I don't cut too deep and puncture any of the intestines.
3. Cut open the belly from the pelvic bone to the breastbone. Do not cut any further if you plan to get your deer mounted.
4. Cut the diaphragm, the membrane separating the chest from the abdomen, from the cavity's walls and work all the way to the spine to separate it.
5. Reach up and into the upper cavity of your deer and grab the windpipe above the lungs and heart. Hold tight and pull it toward you so it's taut. With your other hand, take your knife and carefully reach up, locate the windpipe, and cut it as high up as you can.
6. Remove the heart and the lungs. Remember to save the heart for a delicious meal!
7. Pull the intestines, stomach, and bladder out of the body (at this point they are still connected). Cut coring ring a couple inches (5 to 7.5 cm) deep around the skin and hide surrounding the anus.
8. Pull the stomach and intestines completely out and away from the deer, as now they should be disconnected in one long chain.

Once you're done with the field dressing, it's time to transport your deer back to your home or wherever you plan to continue processing it. Avoid letting dirt, sticks, leaves, and other debris come in contact with the meat.

How to Skin a Deer

When you get your deer back to where you will butcher it, it is ideal to hang the deer using a gambrel (or equivalent). Gambrels have bent legs at each end that are made to hold a deer in the air while you butcher. To hang your deer using a gambrel or a single hook like I used, you will cut an incision through the skin above the joint in the rear legs and stick the gambrel through. It is ideal to hang by the rear legs so that any blood will drain through. I recommend staging the deer somewhere like a garage or other shady area where it will be out of the way and unlikely to attract pests.

You can let the deer age for 2–5 days. As the meat ages, a crust develops on the outer surface, signifying slight decomposition. No worries! The aging process tenderizes and adds flavor as the meat dries, and its connective tissues naturally break down. You will need to keep in mind that you want it at a temperature between 32°F (0°C) and 42°F (5.5°C). Using a walk-in refrigerator is ideal, but not everyone has that luxury. If the temperatures are within that range outdoors, you can simply store the deer in a cool, dry place such as a garage or shop. If the temperature is above that range, there is still a way to properly cool and age your meat. First, you will need to skin your deer for this method and then break down your deer following the "How to Butcher a Deer" section. Once you have your deer divided into quarters and remaining cuts, get out a large cooler. Layer the cooler with ice cubes on the bottom, then a layer of plastic, and then the meat. Repeat the layering as needed. The idea is that the meat should never get wet. Drain this water regularly and change the ice as needed. Flipping the meat and rearranging as often as every 8 hours is necessary for even temperature control. Place the cooler in a shaded place and keep out of direct sun.

In ideal conditions, there are debates whether it is better to leave the hide on your deer before aging it. The choice is yours, but I prefer to leave the skin on because I feel like I waste less (since there is less dried-out meat to remove after aging). Whether you decide to skin the deer before or after aging, you'll follow the same steps:

1. Starting on the inner thigh, use a sharp knife to cut up through the hide just until you reach the knees.
2. Cut through the hide in a circle the whole way around both hind legs and pull the skin away from the meat.
3. Once the skin is loose, you will notice that the skin can be pulled away from the meat without much cutting. Pulling off the skin will prevent you from accidentally cutting the meat, and it also reduces the amount of hair that ends up sticking to the meat.
4. Continue pulling the hide down until you reach the front shoulders.
5. Cut through the hide on the back side of the front legs up to the torso.
6. Pull the hide the rest of the way off the deer to the head.
7. Cut off the head of your deer using a saw. I prefer to leave the roast whole, bone-in, but you can also save the cuts for ground meat. To remove the meat from the neck bone, start at the top and the neck from the chest. Pull the meat from the backstrap incision and skin the meat off the neck bone. You will work this meat from the top of the neck to the deer's windpipe.

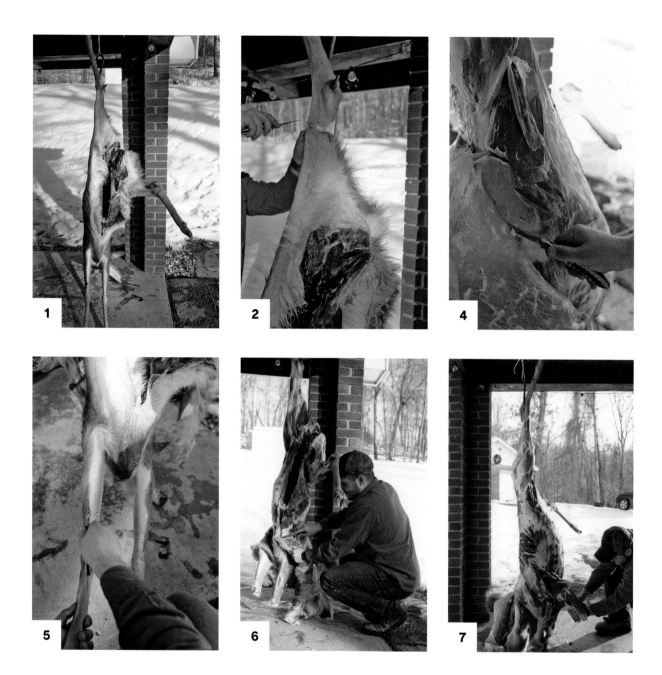

How to Butcher a Deer

There are a handful of different ways on how to butcher your deer. The one thing that remains the same is that there is no greater satisfaction than knowing what happens to your food every step of the process from when it's killed to in your freezer.

1. You will remove the meat from your deer in this order: shoulders, neck, backstraps, tenderloins, rib meat, and then finally, the hindquarters.
2. To begin removing the meat from your deer, you will first remove the two front quarters.
3. Pull the leg away from the torso and use a knife to make cuts into the area where the leg meets the rib cage.
4. Remove the leg completely and repeat the same process on the other side. Set the front legs aside to a clean area.
5. The backstraps are thick pieces of meat along the top edges of the backbone. This is some of the best meat on the deer, so try not to leave any behind. To cut these off, feel for the spine and make an incision down the length of the spine, using the bone as a guide.
6. After you make this lengthwise cut, slowly pull the backstrap away from the bone, loosening it with a knife as you go.
7. The tenderloins are located inside the abdominal cavity and are easy to remove with a few slashes of your knife.
8. The next section is the hindquarters. You'll start at the front of the leg at the knee and make a cut along the bone up to and along the hip.
9. Make a similar cut from the rear portion of the leg to get roasts. There are three distinct groups of muscle. Any smaller pieces of meat that are left can be used however you like. I recommend cubing the meat into chunks that are great for soups or stews.
10. Cut the meat from between the rib bones. This meat is good for grinding into hamburger.
11. Finally, remove the neck. You will pull the meat from the backstrap incision and skin the meat off the neck bone. You will work this meat from the top of the neck to the deer's windpipe.

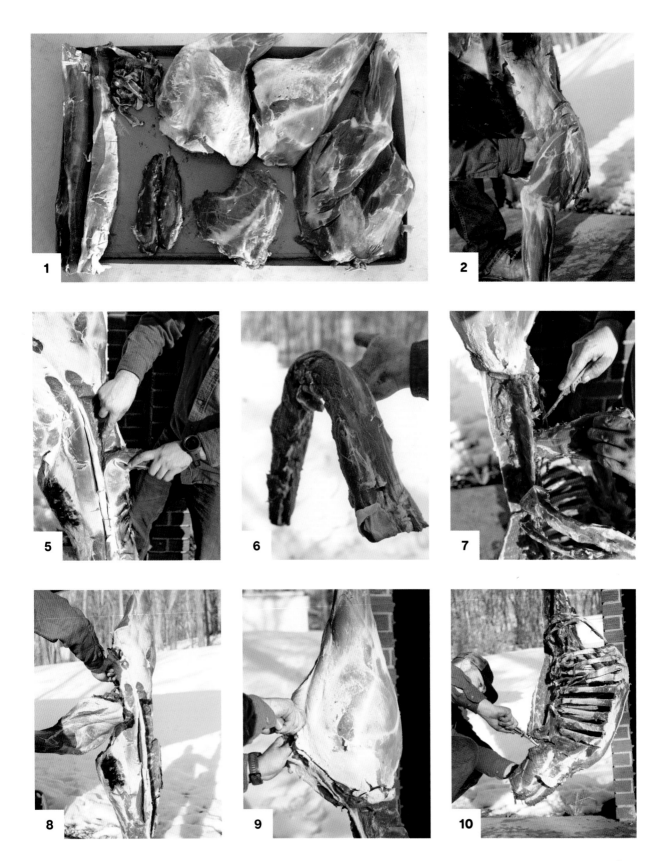

Storing Your Meat

After you've finished your outside work, bring your fresh cuts inside and rinse them well in cold water. Any fat should also be trimmed off. Venison fat, unlike beef fat, is not desirable. It adds to the "gamey" flavor, so it's best to remove it. You can supplement your ground venison with other fatty meats like pork in a 60 to 40 percent ratio of venison to pork. I love the taste of venison and prefer to store my deer as 100 percent venison. Once you have removed any noticeable fat, wrap your venison in freezer paper or place in freezer bags. Mark each package with the type of cut and the year. Properly processed venison can last up to 1 year in the freezer.

1. The shoulders are used for roasts or ground meat. If used as roasts, they should be prepared using a moist, slow-cooking method until tender.
2. The hindquarter offers variability. Its cuts are suitable for steak, jerky, braising, stew, kebabs, and grinding. The major muscles in the hindquarter are the top round, bottom round, eye of round, and sirloin.
3. Shanks, which are the meat from the lower front and rear legs, can be cut into stew meat or ground into burger.
4. Meat trimmed from the deer's neck is typically used for bone-in stews, diced for mincemeat, sliced into strips for jerky, or ground for burger.
5. The tenderloin is the tenderest portion of the deer and is most suitable for steaks. The backstrap also makes for great steaks and can be either frozen whole, cut in half, or cut into fillet pieces.

So there you have it! A step-by-step guide on how to butcher your deer. The first couple times may not be perfect, but you will become more skilled at the process with practice. It's well worth the time to know exactly where your meat is coming from and how it's been handled every step of the way.

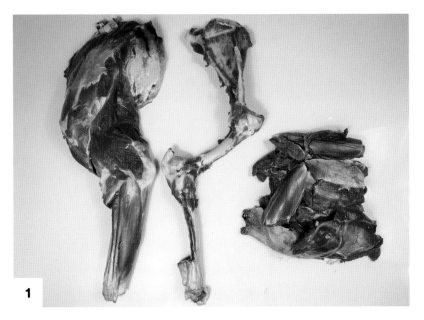

ACKNOWLEDGMENTS

The list of people who have helped me along this journey is endless. I would not be where I am today without the support from my friends, family, and followers on social media. This book would not exist without help from all of you and the endless encouragement I've received.

TO JANE, MY MOTHER:
Thank you for all you have done for me over the years. I owe it to you for starting my love for cooking. Making meals together with you will forever be memories I cherish.

TO DAN, MY FATHER:
Thank you for getting me started in the outdoors and creating the foundation for my favorite hobbies.

TO HUNTER, MY PARTNER:
Thank you for being my recipe tester, my hunting partner, my adventure buddy, and easily my best friend. You have taught me so much over the years about hunting and the outdoors. Without you, I would not be in the position that I am today.

My sisters, my brother, my friends Erin and Kate, and others I forgot to mention: I owe you all a thank-you for helping me make my dreams a reality.

My followers on social media have helped me become a better cook, teacher, and all-around person. I would not have learned or developed into the hunter or chef I am today without your encouragement.

ABOUT THE AUTHOR

JENN DANELLA is a sportswoman, hunter, and wild game chef with a passion for the great outdoors. She was introduced to all things outdoors at a young age by her father—and she still remembers their first fishing trip. She eventually started hunting in high school and soon after, hunting, fishing, and cooking became her full-time passions.

Her goal is to inspire everyone, but women and young adults in particular, to get more involved in outdoor activities. She wants to showcase her own life as proof that women can be a strong asset to the hunting community through their skills and knowledge.

In regard to wild game, Jenn believes it is important to share approachable recipes that celebrate the range of flavors wild game brings to the table. After all, there's no better way to inspire more people to hunt and fish than by demonstrating how delicious it can be! Find her online at www.jenndanella.com.

INDEX

A

alligator tail: Cajun Gator Nuggets, 129

B

bacon
  adding fat with, 19
  California-Style Wild Turkey Sliders, 43
  Rabbit Bourguignon (Rabbit Stewed in Red Wine), 85
  Sweet Heat BBQ Wild Turkey Bites, 51
  Venison and Bacon Breakfast Pizza, 13
  Venison and Irish Stout Sunday Stew, 79
  Venison, Bacon, and Swiss Dip, 37
  Venison Brunch Burger, 19
  Venison Cheeseburger Soup, 75
  Venison Quiche, 15
  Wild Game Tater Tot Casserole, 117
  Wild Hog and Cider Stew, 83
bear: Triple Wild Game Meatballs with Sweet Chili Sauce, 39
biscuits. *See also* burgers; sandwiches; sliders
  Country-Style Biscuits with Venison Gravy, 21
  Honey Butter Pheasant Biscuit, 25–26
burgers. *See also* biscuits; sandwiches; sliders
  Blue Cheese Venison Burgers, 177
  California-Style Wild Turkey Sliders, 43
  Venison Brunch Burger, 19
  Venison Cheeseburger Egg Rolls with Special Sauce, 53
  Venison Cheeseburger Mini Muffins, 49
  Venison Cheeseburger Soup, 75
  Venison Smash Burgers, 147
butchery
  aging, 182
  butchering, 184–185
  field dressing, 181
  "gamey" flavor, 40, 186
  skinning, 182–183
  storage, 186–187

C

casseroles
  Venison Lasagna, 103
  Wild Game Tater Tot Casserole, 117
chili: Venison Chili Mac and Cheese, 105–106

D

dips
  Venison, Bacon, and Swiss Dip, 37
  Wild Hog Queso Verde, 59

duck
  Pan-Fried Duck Dumplings, 127
  Simple Ramen Duck Stir-Fry, 165
dumplings
  Asian Wild Turkey and Pot Sticker Soup, 77
  Pan-Fried Duck Dumplings, 127

E

egg rolls: Venison Cheeseburger Egg Rolls with Special Sauce, 53
enchiladas
  Sunrise Venison Enchiladas, 17
  White Enchiladas with Wild Turkey, 109

F

fat
  adding to wild game, 19
  "gamey" flavor and, 40, 91, 186
  pheasant vs. chicken, 125
  venison vs. beef, 91
  wild hog, 59
field dressing. *See* butchery

G

goose: Smoked Canada Goose Pastrami, 95

H

hunting
  Beretta (beagle), 6, 27
  deer hunting, 144
  Little Katie (lab), 6, 27
  Remington (beagle), 6, 27
  wild turkey hunting, 107

K

kabobs: Chipotle Venison Steak Kabobs, 149

L

lasagna: Venison Lasagna, 103

M

marinades. *See also* sauces
  Apricot-Dijon Glazed Wild Turkey, 151
  game flavor and, 40
  The Go-To Marinade, 144
  Honey Butter Pheasant Biscuit, 25
  Honey Garlic Wild Turkey on a Stick, 157
  Honey Ginger Marinade, 144
  Jamaican Jerk Pheasant, 155
  Rabbit Satay with Peanut Sauce, 61
  Red Wine Marinade, 144

Reverse Seared Rib-Eye of the Sky (Sandhill Crane), 37
Simple Ramen Duck Stir-Fry, 165
Slow-Cooker Garlic-Sesame Venison and Broccoli, 89
Thai Chili Grilled Turkey Lettuce Cups, 153
Umami Marinade, 144
meatballs
  Baked Venison Meatballs with Penne All'Arrabbiata Sauce, 115
  Triple Wild Game Meatballs with Sweet Chili Sauce, 39
muffins: Venison Cheeseburger Mini Muffins, 49

P

pheasant
  Braised French Onion Pheasant, 87
  chicken compared to, 125
  Fried Pheasant Sandwich, 125
  Honey Butter Pheasant Biscuit, 25–26
  Italian Pheasant Noodle Soup, 67
  Jamaican Jerk Pheasant, 155
  Pheasant Fritters with Aioli, 35
pizza
  Barbecue Venison Crescent Ring Pizza, 111
  Venison and Bacon Breakfast Pizza, 13
  Wild Turkey, Tomato, and Mozzarella Flatbread, 45
pot stickers
  Asian Wild Turkey and Pot Sticker Soup, 77
  Pan-Fried Duck Dumplings, 127

Q

quesadillas: Jalapeño Popper Quesadillas with Wild Turkey, 175
quiche: Venison Quiche, 15

R

rabbit
  Lemon Caper Braised Rabbit, 97
  Rabbit Bourguignon (Rabbit Stewed in Red Wine), 85
  Rabbit Satay with Peanut Sauce, 61
rolls
  Barbecue Venison Crescent Ring Pizza, 111
  Spinach and Mushroom Venison Pinwheels, 55
  Venison Cabbage Roll Soup, 73
  Venison Philly Cheesesteaks, 163

S

sandhill cranes: Reverse Seared Rib-Eye
of the Sky (Sandhill Crane), 137
sandwiches. *See also* biscuits; burgers;
sliders
Fried Pheasant Sandwich, 125
Venison Crunchy Wraps, 173
Venison Philly Cheesesteaks, 163
Venison Sloppy Joe Stuffed Grilled
Cheese, 167
sauces. *See also* marinades
Aioli, 35, 129
Arrabbiata Sauce, 115
Bourbon Sauce, 171
Buffalo-Garlic-Barbecue Sauce, 121
Cajun Aioli, 129
Country Gravy, 123
Duck Dumpling Dipping Sauce, 127
Honey Mustard, 57
Meat Sauce, 103
Mustard Sauce, 159
Peanut Sauce, 61
Sloppy Joe Sauce, 167
Special Sauce, 53
Spicy Chimichurri, 139
Stir-Fry Sauce, 165
Sweet Chili Sauce, 39
Sweet Heat Sauce, 51
Thai Chili Mayo, 153
Wild Turkey Cordon Bleu, 119
sliders: California-Style Wild Turkey
Sliders, 43. *See also* biscuits;
burgers; sandwiches
soups and stews
Asian Wild Turkey and Pot Sticker
Soup, 77
Braised French Onion Pheasant, 87
Creamy Wild Turkey and Mushroom
Soup, 71
Green Chile Venison Stew, 81
Italian Pheasant Noodle Soup, 67
Lemon Caper Braised Rabbit, 97
Rabbit Bourguignon (Rabbit Stewed in
Red Wine), 85
Venison and Irish Stout Sunday Stew, 79
Venison Cabbage Roll Soup, 73
Venison Cheeseburger Soup, 75
Venison Stuffed Pepper Soup, 69
Wild Hog and Cider Stew, 83

T

tacos
Slow Cooker Venison Barbacoa, 91
Venison Birria Tacos, 169
Venison Taco Wonton Cups, 47

V

venison backstrap
Chicken Fried Venison, 123
Chipotle Venison Steak Kabobs, 149
Grilled Venison Steak Diane, 161
Reverse Seared Venison Backstrap
with Herb Butter, 141
Venison Philly Cheesesteaks, 163
Venison Steaks with Spicy Chimichurri,
139
Venison with Mustard Sauce, 159
venison, ground
Baked Venison Meatballs with Penne
All'Arrabbiata Sauce, 115
Barbecue Venison Crescent Ring
Pizza, 111
Blue Cheese Venison Burgers, 177
Country-Style Biscuits with Venison
Gravy, 21
Philly Cheesesteak Stuffed Shells, 113
Spinach and Mushroom Venison
Pinwheels, 55
Sunrise Venison Enchiladas, 17
Triple Wild Game Meatballs with
Sweet Chili Sauce, 39
Venison and Bacon Breakfast Pizza, 13
Venison, Bacon, and Swiss Dip, 37
Venison Breakfast Skillet, 23
Venison Brunch Burger, 19
Venison Cabbage Roll Soup, 73
Venison Cheeseburger Egg Rolls with
Special Sauce, 53
Venison Cheeseburger Mini Muffins, 49
Venison Cheeseburger Soup, 75
Venison Chili Mac and Cheese,
105–106
Venison Crunchy Wraps, 173
Venison Lasagna, 103
Venison Quiche, 15
Venison Sloppy Joe Stuffed Grilled
Cheese, 167
Venison Smash Burgers, 147
Venison Stuffed Pepper Soup, 69
Venison Taco Wonton Cups, 47
Wild Game Tater Tot Casserole, 117
venison heart: Pan Fried Deer Heart with
Peppers and Onions, 131
venison roast
Chipotle Venison Steak Kabobs, 149
Green Chile Venison Stew, 81
Slow-Cooker Garlic-Sesame Venison
and Broccoli, 89
Slow Cooker Venison Barbacoa, 91
Venison and Irish Stout Sunday Stew, 79
Venison Birria Tacos, 169
venison tenderloin
Chicken Fried Venison, 123
Marinated Grilled Venison Tenderloin, 143

venison tips and tricks
aging, 182
beef compared to, 91
butchering, 184–185
field dressing, 181
"gamey" flavor, 40, 91, 186
hunting, 144
skinning, 182–183
storage, 186–187
temperature guide, 139

W

wild hog
Chorizo-Inspired Wild Hog Egg Bites, 29
fat content, 59
Green Chile Wild Hog Stew, 81
store-bought pork compared to, 59
Triple Wild Game Meatballs with
Sweet Chili Sauce, 39
Venison Lasagna, 103
Wild Hog and Cider Stew, 83
Wild Hog Queso Verde, 59
wild turkey
Apricot-Dijon Glazed Wild Turkey, 151
Asian Wild Turkey and Pot Sticker
Soup, 77
Bourbon Wild Turkey, 171
Buffalo-Garlic-Barbecue Fried Turkey
Tenders, 121
California-Style Wild Turkey Sliders, 43
Creamy Wild Turkey and Mushroom
Soup, 71
Honey Garlic Wild Turkey on a Stick, 157
hunting, 107
Jalapeño Popper Quesadillas with
Wild Turkey, 175
Pretzel-Crusted Wild Turkey with
Honey Mustard, 57
Slow Cooker Wild Turkey and Stuffing, 93
Sweet Heat BBQ Wild Turkey Bites, 51
Thai Chili Grilled Turkey Lettuce
Cups, 153
White Enchiladas with Wild Turkey, 109
Wild Turkey Cordon Bleu, 119
Wild Turkey, Tomato, and Mozzarella
Flatbread, 45
wraps: Venison Crunchy Wraps, 173